The Black Man on Film

Hayden Film Attitudes and Issues Series
RICHARD A. MAYNARD, Series Editor

The Black Man on Film
Racial Stereotyping

RICHARD A. MAYNARD

Films Editor and Educational Film Reviewer
Scholastic Teacher Magazine

Formerly, Teacher of Social Studies and Afro-American History
Simon Gratz High School, Philadelphia; Community College of
Philadelphia; Great Lakes Colleges Association, Philadelphia

HAYDEN BOOK COMPANY, INC.
Rochelle Park, New Jersey

Library of Congress Cataloging in Publication Data

Maynard, Richard A.   comp.
  The Black man on film: racial stereotyping.

  (Hayden film attitudes and issues series)
  SUMMARY: A high school textbook which discusses the
treatment of minorities, particularly blacks, in
American films.
  "Filmography": p.
  1. Negroes in moving-pictures. [1. Negroes in
motion pictures. 2. Motion pictures] I. Title.
PN1995.9.N4M34   791.43'0909'352   74-4291
ISBN 0-8104-5894-2

Printed in the United States of America

      1   2   3   4   5   6   7   8   9   PRINTING

     74 75 76 77 78 79 80 81 82   YEAR

Editor's Introduction:
Birth of a Stereotype

I am an invisible man. No, I am not a spook like those who haunted Edgar Allan Poe; nor am I one of your Hollywood-movie ectoplasms. I am a man of substance, of flesh and bone, fiber and liquids—and I might even be said to possess a mind. I am invisible, understand, simply because *people refuse to see me.* Like the bodiless heads you sometimes see in circus side shows, it is as though I have been surrounded by mirrors of hard distorting glass. When they approach me they see only my surroundings, themselves or figments of their imagination—indeed, everything and anything except me.

Ralph Ellison, The Invisible Man

HISTORICAL ORIGINS

In his monumental novel, *The Invisible Man,* Ralph Ellison symbolically portrays the frustrating existence of the Black man in White America. To Ellison, the Black man is "invisible" because the American system has denied him an identity. Beginning his experience in this country in the most brutal form of human bondage, the Afro-American has had to adapt his personality to a series of roles, subliminating human desires to challenge his low status in order to survive. This was especially true during slavery when open resistance was punishable by death. Thus, Blacks resorted to a series of tactics designed to make their toil as bearable as possible and to subvert their oppressive masters at the same time. As the slave system crystallized, masters complained bitterly of the "docile," "lazy," "stupid" nature of their Black chattel. Historian John Hope Franklin has explained how the slave himself found that playing the lazy man's role was a shrewd tactic for lightening his burden.

> It must be remembered that some of the manifestations of the slave were superficial and were for the purpose of misleading his owner regarding his real feelings. In this process of adjustment he developed innumerable techniques to escape work as well as punishment, and in innumerable instances he was successful.[1]

---

1.   John Hope Franklin, *From Slavery to Freedom* (New York: Alfred A. Knopf, 1967), p. 206.

However effective, this kind of role playing has, of course, developed into a monolithic, stereotyped image of the Black man in the minds of many Whites. Throughout American history, this image, in turn, has become a generalized expectation for the behavior of Blacks, and it has helped to justify existing feelings of White racism and acts of discrimination.

SOCIAL IMPLICATIONS

Stereotypes are generalizations about groups (ethnic or racial) which tend to create generalized reactions by people toward members of those groups.[2] Concerning Blacks, a standard, stereotyped value judgment would be to make the generalization that "all Blacks are lazy," and then accuse an individual of laziness simply because he's Black.

Stereotypes still present formidable problems in our society despite our belief that we are an enlightened citizenry. The mass media in America—particularly movies and television—compound the negative problems of stereotyping by reflecting these attitudes and reinforcing them over and over again. In his classic study, *The Nature of Prejudice,* Gordon W. Allport states:

> [Stereotypes] are socially supported, continually revived and hammered in, by our media of mass communication—by novels, short stories, newspaper items, movies, stage, radio and television.[3]

Black author, Lawrence Reddick, once noted 19 basic stereotypes of Blacks in American society, all of which he said "supplement each other, though they are sometimes mutually contradictory." His list included:

1. The savage African	11. The unhappy non-white
2. The happy slave	12. The natural born cook
3. The devoted servant	13. The natural born musician
4. The corrupt politician	14. The perfect entertainer
5. The irresponsible citizen	15. The superstitious church-goer
6. The petty thief	16. The chicken and watermelon eater
7. The social delinquent	17. The razor and knife "toter"
8. The vicious criminal	18. The uninhibited expressionist
9. The sexual superman	19. The mental inferior.[4]
10. The superior athlete	

2. Charles F. Marden and Gladys Meyer, *Minorities in American Society* (New York: American Book Company, 1968), p. 33.

3. Gordon W. Allport, *The Nature of Prejudice* (Reading, Mass.: Addison-Wesley Publishing Company, 1954), p. 200.

4. These appear in a footnote to L. D. Reddick's article, reprinted on p. 3 of this book. L. D. Reddick, "Educational Programs for the Improvement of Race Relations: Motion Pictures, Radio, The Press and Libraries," *The Journal of Negro Education* XIII (Summer 1944), p. 369, n.

Most of these prejudiced images have been portrayed in one form or another in our mass media. They are thus vividly reinforced in us, generation after generation. What impact do they have on race relations? What kinds of attitudes do they shape in the minds of White children? What kinds of self-images do they project to young Blacks?

This anthology is designed to serve as a resource book to accompany the viewing of motion pictures, past and recent, which have in some way depicted Blacks in the stereotyped, oversimplified manner described above. Most of the writings contained here are works of protest by Blacks decrying, as Ralph Ellison's "invisible man," the refusal of White America to see them as human beings. As you shall see, this protest is as old as the motion picture medium itself, and it is still continuing today. Each section of this book deals with a different aspect of the problem in chronological order, noting the increasing complexity of the emotions—however irrational—behind the stereotypes. Extracts from several of the key films discussed in this unit are available from Films Incorporated in Wilmette, Illinois on a 30-minute, 16-mm sound film, *The Black Man on Film: Racial Stereotyping.*

As you read through the selections of this book, bear in mind these four fundamental purposes for such a study:

1. to analyze motion pictures as a *mirror* of our social attitudes;
2. to survey, historically, the social impact of films on American race relations;
3. to sensitize ourselves to the legitimate demands of Blacks who, for four decades, have argued for the need to severely alter the cinematic portrayals of their people;
4. to attempt to determine why unrealistic images of minorities persist in our mass media and how we may be able to change them for the future.

Perhaps the best justification for this type of study comes from Lawrence Reddick:

It is an old generalization that equality and full democracy will never be achieved this side of basic changes in the objective conditions of life. To this old maxim must be added another: *democracy in race relations will never be achieved until the minds of people are changed.* The direct route to these minds is through the great agencies of mass communication.[5]

---

5.   *Ibid.,* p. 289.

Contents

PART ONE

Anything But a Man—
A Historical Survey of
the Black Stereotype on Film

In order to appreciate fully the nature of the protest writing which makes up this anthology, a detailed historical background on the Black man in film is necessary. The following three pieces are designed to serve this introductory purpose.

In the first essay, which is an excerpt from his explanation of his satirical play, *Purlie Victorious* (the film version is called *Gone Are the Days*), author, actor, and film director Ossie Davis explains the historical evolution of the Black stereotype in American society. Davis's explanation is demonstrated through an analysis of the character of the Black film actor, Stepin Fetchit, who specialized in stereotyped "darky" roles on the screen for more than twenty years.

The lengthy essays by Lawrence Reddick, former curator of the Schomberg Collection of the New York Public Library (a repository of materials for the study of Black history), and historian Thomas R. Cripps, are historical summaries of the stereotype in detail.

Stepin Fetchit

Ossie Davis

(from "The Wonderful World of Law and Order")

There was a man, who has become synonymous with some of the aspects of our trouble, named Stepin Fetchit. Now, we know that Stepin Fetchit was earning a living; he almost made himself a rich man by caricaturing a certain attitude about Negro people which we know not to be true but which certain people wanted to believe, and this idea was that all Negroes were lazy and stupid and they drawled and said, "Yowsah."

This man was, perhaps, not very bright, and he became a good stereotypical justification of what was wrong with Negroes and why they lived in ghettoes and why they'd never make it. Because they just didn't have it. They were all shiftless. They were all lazy. And they never thought for themselves and always waited for somebody to do something for them. On this basis, we rightly protested the use of Mr. Stepin Fetchit and his character and his talent to demean the whole Negro race, because we realized that the community about us was drawing conclusions from his behavior which we knew to be incorrect and using his behavior to justify the continued oppression in which we found ourselves.

But let's look a little deeper into what originally was behind the meaning of Stepin Fetchit's lazy character. As you will remember, those of you who have a long memory, we were slaves in this country, and we were required to work from sunup to sundown and there was no time off, no coffee breaks, no Social Security, none of the few benefits that we have only lately acquired. Slavery was straight labor, even above and beyond the devotion required of a mule. And we were required, for the benefit of our masters, to work ourselves, literally, to death. If you could—if you were an honest man, an honest Negro, and if you had no way to escape—you would literally work yourself to death, because it was cheaper for a master to work a slave to death and get all the work out of him and later buy a replacement. Now, a slave like Stepin Fetchit, who really was a smart man, who understood the ways of the white folks, would suddenly discover that he was regarded as a very unintelligent creature, so when the master would send him to get a rope he would come back with maybe a plow, until finally the slaveowner would get the idea that this man was so dumb and so inefficient and so shiftless that nothing could be done but to let him sit under a tree.

You might ask why. Why didn't the man take Stepin Fetchit and sell him or get rid of him? Because unconsciously this behavior identified, confirmed and reinforced the slaveowner's prejudices against the possibility of Negroes being responsible, thoughtful and efficient people. So that the Negro achieved two purposes. He saved himself by being too dumb to do the work that the mules and the other slaves were doing, and therefore he survived. And he also gave the overlord the satisfaction of believing that all Negroes were dumb and lazy.

However, I must now protest against the wrong, the invalid use of a stereotype, by whites or by others, after it has been disembodied and the protest content has been removed. Most of the stereotypes we know about Negroes were invented by Negroes for the purposes of survival and social correction. We do this all the time. It is a way in which a society tries to control its members. It will criticize its leaders. It will state its aims, through stereotypes, through jokes and humor. But our humor has been taken away, emptied of its bitter protest content, and has been used against us. And this has led us, sometimes, to rebel against our own humor. In my play *Purlie Victorious,* I have tried to restore the protest content of the Negro's humor.

Educational Programs
for the Improvement of Race Relations:
Motion Pictures

L. D. Reddick

(The Journal of Negro Education, Summer 1944)

INTRODUCTION

The movie, radio, newspaper and library are the most important agencies for the communication of information and ideas in the American society. Together they reach virtually every citizen and present their message to him so often and in such forms that he is powerless to escape it. Through all the arts of suggestion and drama, the manipulation of visual and auditory symbols and the wide use of fascinating entertainment the individual's thoughts and emotions are swept along, directed and redirected according to the prevailing theme. Of more lasting importance is the way basic conceptions are created and molded according to the social pattern.

If the main task of the educative process is the transmission of the culture of the society, then the great educational agencies of the United States are not its schools and colleges; rather, its movie houses, newspapers and magazines, its radio braodcasting stations and its public libraries. Beside them, the formal institutions of learning pale into comparative insignificance. While there are but 30,000,000 persons enrolled in all schools and colleges in the United States, 90,000,000 children and adults attend the movies each week; 30,000,000 homes share with other places the 57,000,000 radio receiving sets, 44,000,000 copies of newspapers are read daily and more than 425,000,000 books are circulated each year to 96,000,000 readers by the public libraries.[1] In a word, what the citizens of this nation think about any broad question is determined, largely, by what these citizens read about it in their newspapers and libraries, hear about it over the radio, or see and hear about it at the movie.

The above observations are fairly commonplace and obvious, yet those individuals and organizations which declare themselves to be interested in improving race relations seem not to realize the decisive influence of these agencies of mass communication in determining public attitudes. Many of the techniques of the race relations betterment organizations have been worked out according to traditional forms of "education" and "converting the *individual* to right thinking." Such methods are incapable of any major influence on the

---

1.   How much more timely this is now, in an age of television.

From *The Journal of Negro Education,* Vol. XIII, Summer 1944. Reprinted by permission of *The Journal of Negro Education* and L. D. Reddick.

public mind. They will continue to lose out in the competition against the propaganda of race hatred and contempt whose proponents have much more quickly appropriated the latest and most effective means of disseminating their message. Here, again, we see the persistence of certain aspects of folk culture in the programs and policies of present-day social action movements. For example, it is scarcely believable but true that not one office of any of the national Negro improvement associations was so much as able to supply a list of anti-Negro films or newspapers or propaganda agencies. No surveys have been made of the impact of these forces on the public mind. Only preliminary thinking has been devoted to the task of drying up the stream of anti-Negro propaganda which pollutes the minds of the people through the major channels of ideas and information.

Accordingly, any evaluation of the movie, the radio, the newspaper and the public library in terms of changing public thinking about the Negro and race relations turns out to be a description of what these four agencies have done to mold such attitudes with a brief note as to possibilities. This procedure is inevitable when so little is to be found of concrete plans to control these instruments of mass communication for the broad social purpose of bettering Negro-white relations.

MOTION PICTURES

Any visitor to neighborhood theatres will testify to their influence. Shouts, laughter, hand-claps, yells and tears are some of the more immediate effects of motion pictures on their audiences. That these experiences, which are often gripping, have an abiding influence is most noticeable in young people. Screen biography, news-reels and travelogues are particularly effective in what they say about history, current events and the peoples and places of the world. The implied associations which are indirectly suggested and repeated by the screen stories often leave residues which are more lasting than the evocative climaxes of the films.

It is, therefore, important to inquire into what such a powerful instrument for influencing the attitudes and behaviour of so many persons has had to say about the Negro. Here we may expect to find one index as to what the American people have come to believe about the Negro, one key to popular stereotypes and the associations linked to them.

A check list of important films shown in the United States which have included Negro themes or Negro characters of more than passing significance reveals that out of this total of one hundred, seventy-five of them must be classified as anti-Negro, thirteen as neutral—with equally favorable and unfavorable scenes—and only twelve as definitely pro-Negro. These measurements, of course, are rough and ready, yet they should be useful enough to indicate the main tendencies. Films are classified as anti-Negro when the Negro elements in them are limited to the stereotyped conceptions of the Negro in the

American mind. Films are classified as pro-Negro when the presentation advances beyond these stereotypes to rôles of heroism, courage and dignity. The overwhelming desire of the Negro people, as expressed through their critics, is to have Negro life admitted to the full range of human characterization, to eliminate the "race linking" of vice and villainies and to have Negro actors on the screen treated "like everybody else."

As everyone knows, most of the films cannot meet this simple test. In them the Negro is exploited chiefly for comic relief. He is the clown, but seldom a magnificent clown; a buffoon; the butt of jokes, not the projector of them, except against himself. He may be an entertainer or a servant, who almost certainly will exhibit some of the following qualities: ignorance, superstition, fear, servility, laziness, clumsiness, petty thievery, untruthfulness, credulity, immorality or irresponsibility with a predilection for eating fried chicken and sliced watermelon. Within these limitations there are all sorts of variations. The Negro elements in films often arise out of situations involving human interest, real humor and drama. There may be excellent acting. However, a rapid review reveals the ceiling above which the Negro on the screen is seldom, if ever,

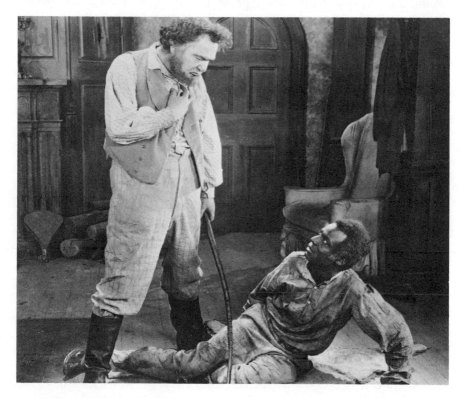

From the motion picture *Uncle Tom's Cabin.* Courtesy of Museum of Modern Art.

permitted to rise. It is significant that this ceiling on the screen is lower than the ceiling for the Negro in American life itself.

The Early Years

Motion pictures as popular entertainment are a Twentieth Century development. Their history may be dated from 1902 when Thomas L. Tully opened the first theatre exclusively for "moving pictures" in Los Angeles. Before 1915, despite constant improvements in technique and a rapidly expanding public interest in this cheap and thrilling amusement, the very best films of those days would be considered quite crude by modern standards. Uneven lighting and the quick, jerky movements and melodramatic gestures of the actors appear amusing now. Yet to contemporary audiences these films were marvelous. Even in these beginning years when the movies were principally "peep shows," the Negro was presented in an unfavorable light. For example, in the prize fights, the Negro pugilist almost invariably was defeated by his white opponent.

In this pre-1915 era were such films of Negro life as the Rastus Series. The very titles of popular favorites like *How Rastus Got His Turkey* and *Rastus Dreams of Zululand* suggest the type of low comedy of these split-reelers. *Coon-town Suffragettes* was quite similar. *For Massa's Sake* tells the story of a devoted slave who wishes to be sold in order to pay the gambling debts of his master. Fortunately, his master discovers a gold mine and things end well before the final fadeout. *In Slavery Days* and *The Octoroon,* both released in 1913, show how tragic it must be for a white person to have a few drops of "Negro blood" in his veins. *The Debt* exploits the same theme with a somewhat original twist: a young man has a white wife and an octoroon mistress. They both have children who, when they have grown up, meet, fall in love and almost marry before they discover their identity. *Uncle Tom's Cabin,* a perennial favorite, was first released as a three-reeler in 1910. The indictment of slavery in the original Harriet Beecher Stowe story was softened so as to make it acceptable to the South. The sight of Jack Johnson knocking out Jim Jeffries, ex-heavyweight champion of the world, was so disturbing to the "race pride" of white audiences and conversely to Negroes as well, that this "prize-fight" film was banned.

The Birth of a Nation

1915 is a great date in film history. This is the year of *The Birth of a Nation,* which in terms of the advancement of the whole technique of presenting life on the screen made it the greatest film ever produced. It was the longest film ever made—twelve reels. It was the first film to be accompanied by a specially arranged orchestral score. It took $100,000 and two years to produce. From the strictly artistic and technical point of view it was a masterpiece of conception and structure. Even today, it is important from this angle. At the same time, *The Birth of a Nation* has remained, without question, the most vicious anti-Negro film that has ever appeared on the American screen. It was based upon the novels of Thomas Dixon, a Negro-phobe Southerner. D. W. Griffith, the film director, was also Southern born. Griffith had decided to call his finished product *The Clansman,* following after the novel. However, at the preview in New York City, Dixon was so impressed and excited that he rose up in the audience and exclaimed to Griffith that the title of so powerful a film should be *The Birth of a Nation.* And so it was.

On March 3, 1915 the picture began its long career of arousing audiences throughout the country. It was a huge financial success. Nobody had ever seen anything like it before. It was the first film to be honored by a White House showing. Afterwards, President Wilson remarked "It was like writing history with lightning." This film spoke to the emotions through the eyes. It showed for all to see that the South was "right" about the Negro, that the North was "right" about preserving the Union, that Reconstruction, which elevated Negroes and some poor whites was a shameful thing, that the virtue of Southern white womanhood had to be protected from "Negro brutes" and that when all seemed lost, the Ku Klux Klan heroically rushed in to save the day. An excellent summary of the social message of this film has been made by Lewis Jacobs:

> The film was a passionate and persuasive avowal of the inferiority of the Negro. In viewpoint it was, surely, narrow and prejudiced. Griffith's Southern upbringing made him completely sympathetic toward Dixon's exaggerated ideas, and the fire of his convictions gave the film rude strength. At one point in the picture a title bluntly editorialized that the South must be made "safe" for the whites. The entire portrayal of the Reconstruction days showed the Negro, when freed from white domination, as arrogant, lustful, villainous. Negro Congressmen were pictured drinking heavily, coarsely reclining in Congress with bare feet upon their desks, lustfully ogling the white women in the balcony. Gus, the Negro servant, is depicted as a renegade when he joins the emancipated Negroes. His advances on Flora, and Lynch's proposal to Elsie Stoneman, are overdrawn to make the Negro appear obnoxious and audacious. The Negro servants who remain with the Camerons, on the other hand, are treated with patronizing regard for their faithfulness. The necessity of the separation of Negro from white, with the white as the ruler, is passionately maintained throughout the film.

In those days, liberals fighting in the cause of the Negro were not too many nor too strong. For example, the National Association for the Advancement of Colored People was but a few years old and in a sense had been founded because public opinion had shown itself to be so indifferent to the abuse of the Negro and the denial to him of elementary rights. Nevertheless, *The Birth of a Nation* was recognized for what it was and was fought. President Charles Eliot of Harvard, Oswald Garrison Villard and Jane Addams were among those who spoke against the film. Rabbi Stephen S. Wise said that *The Birth of a*

Nation was an intolerable insult to the Negro people. Small riots broke out in Boston and a few other communities. The National Association for the Advancement of Colored People sought to have the film banned. Pamphlets and leaflets were issued against it. *The Nation* magazine called the film "improper, immoral and injurious ... a deliberate attempt to humiliate 10,000,000 American citizens and to portray them as nothing but beasts." Dr. Albert Bushnell Hart, well-known historian at Harvard, pointed out the inaccurate and unfair picture given of the Union soldier "intended to leave upon minds the conviction that in Reconstruction time the Negro soldiers freely plundered and abused whites of the South and were encouraged to do so by white officers." D. W. Griffith, the film producer, rose to its defense with a pamphlet entitled *The Rise and Fall of Free Speech in America,* which included copious quotations from leading newspapers and magazines which had endorsed the film.

All of this public commotion was a great boon to the box office. The film was banned in less than a dozen cities. The most objectionable scenes were "cut" in several other places. Since the movement was not at all strong enough to prohibit the showing of the film, it served as a great advertisement to thousands who otherwise might have never heard of it. This is not unusual in the history of social action programs. Nevertheless, for the first time the American people began to realize the power of the movie for social suggestion and for influencing life itself. *The Birth of a Nation* was popular for a decade and doubtlessly did incalculable damage to race relations. Its glorification of the Ku Klux Klan was at least one factor which enabled the Klan to enter upon its period of greatest expansion, reaching a total membership of 5,000,000. Present-day attempts to revive the film usually have been beaten back by Negro, liberal and radical groups. Revival showings today cut out the Reconstruction scenes, which are the most offensive.

The Talkie

The next great turning point in the development of the movie as a popular art form came in 1927 when the *Jazz Singer* made it clear that the "talking picture" would be the movie of the future. Al Jolson, in black-face, sang his songs well and captivated his audiences with the naturalness of his speaking voice. Definitely, a new dimension had been added to this form of mass entertainment. Between *The Birth of a Nation* and the *Jazz Singer* were about two dozen films with important Negro characters or scenes. About all of these followed the usual pattern. None, save *Free and Equal,* even attempted to approach *The Birth of a Nation* in a direct appeal to race hatred. *Free and Equal* was a cheap imitation of the real thing. It failed miserably in its attempt to capitalize upon the popularity of the anti-Negro-equality theme. *The Nigger* was more objectionable in title than in content. It was an adaptation of Edward Sheldon's novel, *The Governor.* With one or two exceptions, films between 1915 and 1927, when they treated the Negro at all, adhered to the stereotypes.

The movie industry experienced a great expansion as a result of the introduction of the "talkie." Since Negroes are generally accredited with highly musical voices, it might be expected that this new medium of sound would open up new opportunities to them in Hollywood. In a sense this was true. In the period from 1927 to 1939 (when the next great anti-Negro picture was produced), the number of Negro parts in Hollywood films greatly increased. Let us see how often the stereotypes were departed from.

There was, to begin with, the *Our Gang* comedies of child life. This series was first started back in the days of the silent film. Comparatively speaking, their record for fair play was well above the average. Some of the films may be classified as pro-Negro in that the humor and pathos which come to children were presented without any "race angling." The children were not separated. They played together, easily and naturally, though in some of the films there was a tendency to place the Negro child in a somewhat more ridiculous or subservient position. The Negro child actors, with one exception, were brilliant and winsome. Even now film fans speak with enthusiasm of "Sunshine Sammy," "Farina" and "Stymie." "Buckwheat" did not come off so well nor was he (or she) so well cast. Occasionally, Negro movie fans would protest about a line here or a situation there, but on the whole, *Our Gang* maintained itself as one of Hollywood's few contributions to better Negro-white relations.

Another attempt of Hollywood to do better by the Negro may be noted in one of the all-Negro features which appeared in 1929. King Vidor, with appropriate newspaper flourishes, produced *Hallelujah.* This was his first talking picture. It was also the first, Hollywood-produced, all-Negro feature. Technically, it registered certain advances; sociologically, there may be some doubt. Nina Mae McKinney and Daniel Haynes were the stars. The scenes were laid in the cotton fields and city dives of the South. There was the eternal struggle between good and evil as symbolized by a man of God and a woman of the devil. Naturally, this gave many opportunities for preaching, shouting, baptizing, soul saving, spiritual singing, dancing, gambling, love-making and general good times. A double premiere for the film was held in New York City at the Astor theatre downtown and the Lafayette Theatre in Harlem. Most of the reviewers and the daily press liked *Hallelujah.* Some of the Negro newspaper critics did, too. W. E. B. DuBois, usually hard to please, said that it was "beautifully staged under severe limitations . . . a sense of real life without the exaggerated farce and horseplay, . . . marks *Hallelujah* as epoch-making." However, there were those who disagreed. Letters to the editor spoke of King Vidor's "filthy hands reeking with prejudice." Another commentator referred to *Hallelujah's* "insulting niggerisms." Almost everyone seemed to like that "sweet little copperish brownskin," Nina Mae McKinney.

Hallelujah was significant in that it gave Negro actors important rôles and did not exhibit the crude insults which disturbed Negro patrons; however, it did not advance very far beyond the usual stereotypes and, as everyone could see, being all-Negro was by that token a jim crow film. It was a box-office failure.

Did it fail because the producers were too timid or because they themselves were prisoners of the popular stereotypes of the Negro? If they believed the stereotypes were true, when they attempted to tell "the truth" they still portrayed stereotypes. One historian of the American movie had this to say:

> In undertaking *Hallelujah,* Vidor also said he was primarily interested in showing the Southern Negro as he is. The deed fell short of the intent. The film turned out, however, to be a melodramatic piece replete with all the conventionalities of the white man's conception of the spiritual-singing, crapshooting Negro.

During this same year another all-Negro feature was presented to the public by Hollywood. This was *Hearts in Dixie.* Stepin Fetchit was the star. His great art was used to drive in deeper than ever the stereotype of the lazy Negro good-for-nothing.

The two most controversial "Negro films" of this period were *Emperor Jones* and *Imitation of Life.* Paul Robeson was the star in the screen version of Eugene O'Neill's play. With few exceptions, critics in the daily press praised this as one of the best films of the year. The Negro critics were divided. Some thought that it was well that a Negro emperor should be shown and that a white man, for the first time, could be presented on the screen as his lackey. Others, however, emphasized the pullman porter, chain-gang and voodoo scenes. Before the final act, Robeson, the Emperor, is grovelling on his belly in the spirit-infested jungle. *The Chicago Defender* carried Robeson's picture under the caption "Attacked by Film Fans." One writer charged O'Neill and Hollywood with the purpose of presenting the Negro as "essentially craven."

The controversy over *Imitation of Life* came to such a point that Fannie Hurst, the author of the novel by the same name, and Sterling Brown, who was then writing criticism for *Opportunity* magazine, were the principals in a clash of opinion. In criticism of the self-effacing Negro character, Brown wrote: "once a pancake, always a pancake."[2] Fannie Hurst thought that Negroes should be a little more grateful for the "break" which she had given them in her novel and which carried over into the screen story. Editorials in the Negro press were rather unanimous in their praise of Louise Beavers and Fredi Washington as actresses, but they expressed annoyance and disgust at many scenes. In one of these Miss Beavers tells her former mistress that she does not wish to take her share of the profits from their joint pancake business and move into a home of her own; rather, true to the role of the devoted servant, she desires to remain "on the premises" to serve her white "ma'am" and "to rub your little feet every night when they are tired, just like I always used to do." Apparently, all the ex-Negro maid wanted for herself was a big funeral with white horses. "Peola," the name of the maid's mulatto daughter who either wanted to be white or, at least, enjoy all of the privileges which the daughter of the white woman enjoyed,

2.   For complete article, see pp. 49–51 of this volume.

became for a time a widely used term in Negro conversation. The comment of the *Literary Digest* was quoted with approval by many Negro newspapers:

> The real story, the narrative which is merely hinted at, never really contemplated, is that of the beautiful and rebellious daughter of the loyal Negro friend. She is light-skinned, sensitive, tempestuous; she grows bitterly indignant when she sees that the white girl with whom she has been reared is getting all the fine things of life while she is subjected to humiliation and unhappiness.

> Obviously, she is the most interesting person in the cast. Her drama is the most poignant, but the producers not only confine her to a minor and carefully handled subplot, but appear to regard her with a bit of distaste. They appear to be fond of her mother, because she is the meek type of old-fashioned Negro that, as they say, "knows his place," but the daughter is too bitter and lacking in resignation for them.

Space prohibits more than a bare mention of many other films. The favorable Negro films make a short list. Among them were *Arrowsmith*, which included Clarence Brooks as a dignified Negro doctor in the West Indies (a reviewer for the Associated Negro Press termed this "the best legitimate part ever allotted to a colored actor in the history of the movies"); *Flying Down to Rio*, in which Etta Moten sang and a chorus danced the "Carioca"; *The Spirit of Youth* which told the story of the life of Joe Louis and *The Singing Kid* in which Cab Calloway and Al Jolson pal about on equal terms before Calloway and his band render their musical numbers.

Huckleberry Finn, with Rex Ingram in the "Nigger Jim" rôle, did show the passionate wish for freedom on the part of the runaway slave and the human response to this sentiment on the part of the unspoiled youngster. *Dark Rapture* was one of the few authentic films of Africa to reach the commercial theatre houses.

The films unfavorable to the Negro make a long list. There were, for example, the *March of Time* news-reels on Harlem voodoo and Father Divine; various Stepin Fetchit pictures like *Judge Priest* and *Carolina* (with Hattie McDaniels); various Bill Robinson pictures like *The Little Colonel, The Littlest Rebel* and *Steamboat 'Round the Bend;* various Clarence Muse pictures like *So Red the Rose,* in which one little white Southern girl from the big house routs a plantation insurrection by slapping the face of one of the Negro insurrectionists. Louis Armstrong appears in Bing Crosby's haunted house cafe in *Pennies From Heaven. King Kong* and *Baboona* were typical African films with the usual emphasis upon the naked, "primitive," black savages who consider every blonde a goddess and every trader or missionary a god. These African films sometimes went so far as to show an animal absconding with a native woman or actually eating a native man as in *When Africa Speaks. Trader Horn,* though ambitious and expensive, was pointed out to be false and misleading. In *The Green Pastures,* another all-Negro feature, Hollywood turned the rather majestic and dignified play into a light and, for the most part, ridiculous travesty. In *Show Boat* Paul Robeson got a chance to do some magnificent singing. However, he was merely a roustabout with the maid-cook Hattie McDaniels as his wife. "Moran and Mack" continued the stereotyped black-face minstrel tradition with *Hypnotized.*

The Era of Gone With The Wind

With *Gone With The Wind,* the creation of a motion picture became a national event. Already the country had "gone wild" over the novel. By 1939, the year the film was made, more than 2,000,000 copies of the book had been sold. When to this were added reprints, cheap editions and serialized versions, it meant that half the book-reading public in the United States had read Margaret Mitchell's super "best-seller." It was advertised in the *American Historical Review* as the greatest historical novel ever written by an American.

This wide interest was kept at fever heat by skillful publicity. Hollywood's search for a suitable Scarlett O'Hara lasted for a year, brought forth thousands of candidates and finally ended up with the selection of an English actress, Vivian Leigh. When the filming actually began there was some sensational or intriguing story about it each week, to keep the public interest from lagging. Before the production was completed, some two years and $3,700,000 had been spent. The great day came on Thursday, December 14, 1939. All eyes turned to Atlanta, Georgia—sometimes called the capital of the South—for the long awaited world premiere. Below the Mason and Dixon line it was a day of glory. For Atlanta it was more than a holiday. Confederate flags and the festival spirit pervaded the town. Several governors of neighboring states were on hand. Newspapers editorialized at length and published corrected versions of the "Rebel Yell."

The South was right. *Gone With The Wind* said in the most effective manner possible that the Ante-Bellum South, that wondrous land of beauty and happy slaves, had been destroyed by Union soldiers and carpet-baggers. The Negroes in the film, as in the novel, did not want to be free. They were shown as liars, would-be rapists, mammies and devoted field hands. All of this was so inter-woven with the story, presented so beautifully in technicolor, with all of the arts of sight and sound coordinated, that the effect on the unsuspecting patron was irresistible.

The parallels with *The Birth of a Nation* are instructive. Both were about the South, the Civil War and the Negro. Both were remarkable films from the artistic and technical point of view, though *Gone With The Wind* was a bit too long (3 hours; 45 minutes) and the last half was less competent than the first half. Both were huge financial successes—as early as 1940 it was estimated that *Gone With The Wind* would gross $60,000,000. Both were great as anti-Negro propaganda, but differed in their approaches. While *The Birth of a Nation* was direct, *Gone With The Wind* was subtle. The social consciousness of the nation had developed to such a point that the inflammatory appeals of 1915 were not permissible in 1939. Perhaps there was little need for the former obviousness. The art of suggestion had matured.

Some critics felt that where *The Birth of a Nation* ended, *Gone With The Wind* began. The latter completed the job of wiping out of the public mind the "Northern" view of slavery, Civil War and Reconstruction, replacing it with the traditional "Southern" view. Ideologically the South had won the Civil War. The defeat which it suffered on the field of battle was more than repaired by its victory over the minds of the American people through history books, novels, and now the motion pictures. Some critics felt that the final touch to this victory came with the award to Hattie McDaniels of an "Oscar" from the Academy of Motion Picture Arts and Sciences for her rôle as "Mammy."

Despite the triumph of the film, a vigorous fight was waged against it. During the production period the National Association for the Advancement of Colored People and other groups were successful in getting some of the most offensive scenes eliminated or, as in some instances, softened. The film as finally released was not as bad as the novel. Perhaps these concessions were the reasons that the NAACP did not lead or even join in the fight against the showing of the finished product. This fight was led by groups like the National Negro Congress, certain Negro newspapers and "left" political groups. The *Socialist Appeal* denounced the film as a glorification of the old South. Virtually all of the other radical groups did likewise. But it was the Communist Party which carried on the most consistent struggle against it. To begin with, the motion picture reviewer who refused to expose the anti-Negro bias of the film was fired from the staff of the *Daily Worker.* Editorials, articles, cartoons in this newspaper and in the *New Masses* blasted *Gone With The Wind* as "vicious," "reactionary," "inciting to race hatred," "slander of the Negro people," and "justifying Ku Klux Klan."

Negro leaders in Harlem, Brooklyn, other Northern cities and in a few Southern communities condemned the film. The National Negro Congress issued news releases and hand bills and joined with other Negro and "left" groups to picket theatres where the film was shown. Some trade unions and units of the American Labor Party in New York supported these moves. This large effort to have the film banned, withdrawn or boycotted was altogether unsuccessful, even in Negro neighborhoods. But it did serve to further "educate" the public to something of an awareness of anti-Negro elements in motion pictures and the power of the movie for developing social attitudes.

The net effect of such a film on the public mind can only be guessed. Walter White himself said that whatever sentiment there was in the South for a Federal anti-lynch law, evaporated during the *Gone With The Wind* vogue. At least one Southern child, who had seen the film, is reported to have told his Negro nurse-maid that this servant would still be a slave and "Daddy would not have to pay you" but for the Yankees.

Since Gone With The Wind

Since 1939 the story of the Negro in motion pictures must be summarized and telescoped. Generally speaking, from the Negro angle, the films have improved. Some of the most objectionable ones were like *The Texan* and *Santa Fe Trail.* In the former a lone, drunken Negro in the uniform of the Union Army staggers down the street of a Southern city during the Reconstruction period and blurts out "Gangway for the United States Army." In the latter the abolitionist hero, John Brown is transformed into an inhuman fanatic. In the *Prisoner of Shark Island,* one unarmed white man audaciously approaches Negro troops with guns pointed toward him and commands, "Put that gun down, Nigrah!" And the Negroes, true to Hollywood, say to themselves, "He means it. He's no Yankee. He's a Southern white man." Obediently, they put their guns down.

Mr. Washington Goes to Town was advertised as the first all-Negro feature comedy. Its general tone may be indicated by the confession of one character in the film that "pork-chops is the fondest thing I is of." *Tennessee Johnson* was fought by the National Negro Congress, "left" groups and trade unions as being anti-Negro and anti-democracy in the sense that it glorified President Andrew Johnson and his cooperation with the "Southern Bourbon aristocracy." This film, too, was modified at the suggestion of the NAACP prior to its release and again the NAACP declined to join in the public fight against it. However, more other-than-Negro support for the fight against this film was mobilized than ever before. Perhaps this was largely responsible for the box-office failure of this production.

Fury and *The Ox-bow Incident* are two of the few American-made films which show the lynch mob. These represent high points for Hollywood courage. This courage, however, is not unlimited. For example, in *Fury* there is no Negro. In *The Ox-bow Incident* there is a Negro but he is not the lynch victim, nor does the lynching take place in the South. Nevertheless, the lynch spirit is shown. It is not glorified. As a matter of fact, the symbolism is so skillful in *The Ox-Bow Incident* that the leader of the mob is a Southerner, and the lone Negro in the story—Leigh Whipper—is shown to be on the side of "justice, humanity and civilization." Incidentally, Whipper had a rôle of similar importance, calling forth sympathy and understanding, in *Of Mice and Men. Proud Valley* (also known as *The Tunnel*) is unusual in that a Negro appears as the star of a film in which all the other actors are white. However, the locale is not the United States nor are there any love scenes which involve him. Instead, the Welsh miners do a great deal of singing and digging in the mines. Robeson, the star, comes off well. Altogether this is a great step forward for the film industry.

Young Pushkin, produced in Russia, was the straight story of the early life of Alexander Pushkin, the Russian poet of part Negro ancestry. This story was told without the slightest "race" consciousness. No American film has ever reached this height. The three American-made films which perhaps came nearest to it were: *In This Our Life, Bataan* and *Sahara. Arrowsmith*, produced back in 1931, is about the only other Hollywood film which goes into their class. All of these depart from the stereotypes.

In *In This Our Life* (Warner Brothers), an earnest, truthful, energetic Negro lad, speaking perfect English, refuses "to take the rap" for the wreckless, neurotic, Southern belle, who, in a fit of temper (her sister's husband did not keep the rendezvous with her), runs down a child with her automobile. The Negro boy, despite threats and bribes, refuses to "Uncle Tom." Instead, he "talks back" and airs the Negro problem with courage and dignity. Incidentally, this Negro boy is presented as a clerk and law student—not, as usual, a cotton-picker or a tap-dancer. This picture won a place on the Honor Roll of Race Relations for 1942. *Bataan* told the story of last ditch stand there of American soldiers against the Japanese enemy. There is a Negro soldier—Kenneth Spencer—who is drawn as naturally and sympathetically as are any of his half-dozen companions. They all behave like men. The NAACP presented an award to Warner Brothers for this creditable production. In *Sahara* (Columbia) the French Negro soldier—Rex Ingram—is handsome. He is perhaps the first Negro on the screen who has been permitted to have a white man as his personal servant—a captured Italian soldier. The Negro soldier is allowed to be brave and intelligent. He uses his hands as a cup for the dripping water which quenches the thirst of the whole group. As a climax this Negro, in the face of gun-fire, overtakes a fleeing Nazi, physically overcomes him and pushes his blonde head down into the desert sand. This may be the first time ever that any Negro—even a foreign Negro—has been permitted by Hollywood to assume a heroic rôle while killing a white man, even an enemy.

Four all-Negro films illustrate another positive, though limited, development. *Dr. George Washington Carver* was a feature built around the life and work of the scientist. Not a first-rate production, yet it was important historically. It has been reported that at least one Hollywood studio is interested in a full-length story of Carver's life. *Cabin in the Sky* exhibited the stereotypes, yet these were softened considerably. For example, the line "eating fried chicken all the time" was deleted from the theme song of the film. The Negro couples who dance and sing do so with grace and restraint. They are attractive couples. When the inevitable brawl occurs in the cabaret, the participants fight with guns and not with the traditional razors. Lena Horne, here as elsewhere, is permitted to be a beautiful girl. Ethel Waters is given a chance to do some real acting and the jokes are not necessarily derogatory to the Negro. *Stormy Weather* was one of those great star-studded musicals. It contained no particular indignities, though, again, the Negro is an entertainer. Within this limitation, all sorts of talents are displayed. Especially noteworthy are the dances of the Nicholas Brothers and Katherine Dunham. However, this film, like all other Negro films, is jim-crow. In that sense it is false and objectionable. . . .

Pattern of Change

Thus, from these brief notes the social function of the movie in the realm of race relations should be clear. The following generalizations seem to be justified:

1. That the Negro is usually presented as a savage or criminal or servant or entertainer.
2. That the usual rôles given to Negro actors call for types like Louise Beavers, Hattie McDaniels, "Rochester," Bill Robinson, Clarence Muse and various jazz musicians.
3. That other groups such as Orientals, Mexicans and South Europeans are sometimes presented unfavorably, but no religious or racial minority is so consistently "slandered" as the Negro.
4. That films have improved somewhat during the present war.[3]
5. That when an attempt is made to improve the treatment of the Negro on the screen, the improvement usually takes place within the limitations of an all-Negro film.
6. That these limitations on the Negro are also important as limitations on the development of the movie as an art form and as an organ of democratic culture.

The testimony is virtually unanimous from those who are aware of the treatment of the Negro by the movie that such portrayal is inaccurate and unfair. Directly and indirectly it establishes associations and drives deeper into the public mind the stereotyped conception of the Negro. By building up this unfavorable conception, the movies operate to thwart the advancement of the Negro, to humiliate him, to weaken his drive for equality and to spread indifference, contempt and hatred for him and his cause. This great agency for the communication of ideas and information, therefore, functions as a powerful instrument for maintaining the racial subordination of the Negro people.

If all this is true, it goes without saying that any real program of correcting the mistreatment of the Negro by the movie industry must include basic changes in the social order of which the movies are a part. But more immediately and directly such a program would surely need to consider:

1. The use of non-commercial movies which treat the Negro favorably. There are any number of worthwhile films which have been produced or distributed by government agencies, labor unions, film libraries or other educational institutions. The entertainment qualities of this type of film are being constantly improved. Churches, schools, libraries, clubs, YMCA's and other organized groups could make wide use of these inexpensive shows.

3.   World War II.

2. Production of more and better films by Negroes themselves. Frankly, most of the movies made by Negro producers have been of third-rate quality. Yet the success of Oscar Micheaux with his melodramas suggest what could be done if those who know better would help.

However, the main effort must be concentrated on the commercial film—Hollywood. The question has been asked many times: why does Hollywood treat the Negro so. As the *New York Age* put it, "When will Hollywood producers have the guts and moral courage to give a true-to-life version of Negro characters when they are intimately associated with white characters?" The first answer may be that most of the Hollywood producers believe that they are presenting the Negro "as he is." But beyond this superficial naïveté, it is to be remembered that the movie industry is a money-making business. It has been said that Hollywood will produce anything that it can get away with *that will sell.* This may be an extreme generalization, but one important executive of the movie industry himself has said:

> We are in the game to make money, not to make friends or enemies. We produce whatever it pays to produce, regardless of color or creed of the subjects. In order to realize adequate profits on a production distribution must be nation-wide. It does not suffice that the East, West and North accept Negro pictures, and the South refuses to accept pictures wherein Negroes are starred.

And the South does insist upon the color line upon the screen. There have been Southern associations against "social equality" on the screen. Some of these, like the Southern Film Association, go so far as to object to all-Negro films like *Hallelujah* since Negroes are the stars in them.

The strategy of those working for better treatment of the Negro, accordingly, must be worked out in terms of the profit motive of the industry. Hollywood will respond to the proper pressures just like everything else does. . . .

The Death of Rastus:
Negroes in American Films Since 1945

Thomas R. Cripps

Hollywood and any national film industry for that matter is both a leader
and a follower of public opinion. In portraying foreign characters it
reflects what it believes to be the popular attitudes of the time, but it also
turns these often vague attitudes into concrete images.[1]

Thus in American motion pictures in-group self-images will become the norm of
behavior and all the jangling diversity of ethnic groups will round off into a
broadly based white Anglo-Saxon Protestant type. Some minority groups have
contributed to this kind of negative stereotyping by their protests against
reprehensible typing. Witness protests by Italians against *The Untouchables* and
protests by Negroes against *The Birth of a Nation.* The result is not an
elimination of the stereotypes but instead the continuation of the least
objectionable of them. As Terry Ramsaye stated: "the multitude can chuckle at
Step'n Fetchit and laugh with Rochester, but they will woo and win with the
Gables, the Taylors and the Coopers." Thus villainous Negroes stay off the
screen at the price of making "the negro [sic] so amusing and agreeable that an
audience is always pleased at the appearance of a black face."

    The combination of these two factors produces a kind of selective
censorship. The history of film censorship in America is a long, tedious tale of
the suppression of the sins of the Puritans. As Sterling Brown has pointed out,
seven stereotypes of Negroes can be isolated: the contented slave, the wretched
freeman, the comic Negro, the brute Negro, the tragic mulatto, the local color
Negro, and the exotic primitive. The elements of these types include laziness,
filth, sensuality, and crime, so that it is as though white America is torn between
two conclusions: Negroes are America's anti-democratic nightmare and Puritan
conscience and must be suppressed, or they must be depicted publicly as the
stereotype because it sustains the myth of Anglo-Saxon purity.

    In practice a compromise has been struck. The private censorship code of
the motion picture producers of America proscribes all the vicious elements of
the stereotype and tolerates the ridiculous elements. Thus, through the 1930's
and 1940's, only racial comics such as Rochester, Willie Best, and Mantan
Moreland (as Charlie Chan's valet) crept into American films. The effect in
recent films has been that Negroes must still remain segregated even as the
imperatives of segregation diminish in reality. A normal sexual role, for example,
continues to be denied to Negroes [as of 1967]. Sidney Poitier, in the widely

1.   Siegfried Kracauer, "National Types as Hollywood Presents Them," **Public
      Opinion Quarterly,** XIII, 1 (Spring, 1949), 53–72.

From **Phylon,** Vol. 28, 1967. Reprinted by permission.

acclaimed *Lilies of the Field,* is as effectively denied a full characterization by the presence of the nuns as co-stars as, say, Lena Horne was in the musicals in which she was consigned to a vaudeville act that bore no relation to the plot line. . . .

It can be seen that although movies are a "symbolic expression of life," they can shape "value patterns" to a degree only and then not in the efficient way assumed by the earlier observers.

Socially conscious Hollywood producers have accepted this view to some extent. Many are self-conscious and guilty about the charge that Hollywood's achievements in race relations over the long run have been anti-Negro from *The Birth of a Nation* to *Gone With the Wind.* But it would be difficult to imagine a different condition in view of the social scientists' vision of moviemakers as essentially followers of rather than creators of mores. They would have had to crusade, "which Hollywood seldom does except for the most certain and established causes."

Censorship has been one of the most persistent influences on the maintenance of stereotypes. Southern censorship has taken the most exaggerated stances. In Atlanta, *Lost Boundaries* and *Imitation of Life* were banned *in toto* as inciting to violence or lawbreaking. Of all the movies in the 1940's about Negroes only Faulkner's *Intruder in the Dust* was uncut. In 1945 *Brewster's Millions* was banned in Memphis because Eddie Anderson stood too close to, and seemed too friendly with, Helen Walker. Even an innocuous film such as *Island in the Sun* was either protested or banned in Memphis, New Orleans, Jacksonville, and Montgomery, because White Citizens Councils and the Ku Klux Klan saw it as "immoral and indecent" because of the implied equality of the characters of Harry Belafonte and Joan Fontaine. . . .

The story of Negroes in American films since 1945, therefore, is not only the story of the death of Rastus, or Sambo, or Uncle Tom, but the rebirth of a complete man as yet unnamed. The story, so far, has three parts: up to 1954, Negroes as a social problem; through the 1950's, Negroes as emerging characters yet bearing the vestiges of Rastus; and finally from the varied themes of the 1960's, the beginnings of the fully articulated character. The first intimations of the end of the Negro stereotype were seen in the anti-fascist war movies: Dooley Wilson's wise piano player in Warner Brothers' *Casablanca;* Rex Ingram's Senegal soldier in *Sahara;* and Canada Lee in Alfred Hitchcock's *Lifeboat.*

Shortly after the vogue of war movies ended, the cycle of racial message movies began. Stanley Kramer's *Home of the Brave,* adapted from Arthur Laurents' polemic against anti-Semitism, was the first in 1948, followed by Louis de Rochemont's *Lost Boundaries* and Elia Kazan's *Pinky.* By 1952, with Clarence Brown's *Intruder in the Dust* the cycle had spent itself, not so much departing from the old stereotypes but creating a new one: that of Negroes who cannot be fulfilled without the sacrifice of or the support of white men. As a case in point, James Edwards, the Negro in *Home of the Brave,* goes on a mission to a Japanese-held island where his best friend, a white man, is killed. Edwards feels a dual guilt at his friend's death first, because he is glad that he personally survived and second, because he had wished his friend dead after an argument in which he had been called a racial epithet. Falling victim to hysterical paralysis, he is taken to the base psychiatrist who induces Edwards to walk again by hurling the same epithets at him, symbolically implying that Negroes can be fulfilled only on white men's terms. At the end of the film the audience sees a fraternal scene in which Edwards and a one-armed white man depart, suggesting Negro-white equality only as long as the whites are not complete. In *Pinky, Lost Boundaries,* and *Intruder in the Dust* the problems by Negroes are resolved in each case at the pleasure of upper-class white society. So little came from the cycle of problem movies that Negroes nearly disappeared from the screen completely in the early 1950's.

By the mid-1950's the cycle had achieved only a few side effects. The all-Negro exploitation films such as Robert Gordon's *Joe Louis Story* and James Wong Howe's *Go Man Go,* a cheap program movie about the Harlem Globe Trotters, declined in numbers. The South's romantic "lost cause" mystique became tarnished and its decadence in the manner of Tennessee Williams was emphasized in a rash of movies. Indians began to get sympathetic treatment in several Westerns.

After 1954, cinema Negroes became, not a problem for whites to comprehend, but symbolic figures of the struggle against oppression. In the strident *Blackboard Jungle,* only Sidney Poitier is allowed to struggle successfully against the tide of urban poverty. In Darryl Zanuck's movie of Alec Waugh's *Island in the Sun,* it is Harry Belafonte, until then a popular nightclub singer, who plays the dynamic labor leader; and in Robert Wise's tightly directed crime thriller, *Odds Against Tomorrow,* it is again Belafonte who is the criminal at war with both society and his Southern racist accomplice. Only occasionally did the old Negro intrude upon the new Negro tragic hero-as-victim, as in Otto Preminger's gaudy proudction of *Porgy and Bess* in 1959.

By the 1960's, institutional racial equality had become socially acceptable behavior in many areas of America. One heard occasional liberal voices even from a closed society such as Mississippi. Churches began to break their long silence on the issue of race. Professional associations opened their doors to Negroes. No longer news was the marriage of the famous Negro actor, Sammy Davis, Jr.; nor Lyndon Johnson, late of Texas, dancing at his inauguration with the wives of the various darker-skinned men in attendance. Such rapid change was accepted in varying degrees. The intellectuals and the well-to-do had nothing to fear from it. The middle-class houseowner nervously accepted it in every neighborhood but his own. Older people and working-class people tended to not accept it at all. These varying degrees of acceptance of change were reflected in a tripartite cinema of the 1960's. A comparable case can be seen in the film treatment of juvenile behavior in the highly literate *David and Lisa* by Frank and Eleanor Perry; the middle-brow, guilt-evoking *Rebel Without a Cause;* and the sensational exploitation movie, *Untamed Youth;* each one dealing with the same subject, but in three distinct styles. Similarly, as Negroes intrude upon the collective consciousness of America they evoke a similar set of divergent images.

At the lowest level of exploitation of racial themes is Stephen Borden's *My Baby is Black,* which depicts a love affair between a Negro medical student in Paris and his white girl friend. The audience is titillated by shots of the two in embrace alternated with scenes of vicious rejection of the Negro by the girl's parents. Another cheap exploitation film of the 1960's was Larry Buchanan's *Free, White, and 21,* in which a Negro, Frederick O'Neal, is accused of rape and acquitted. The film's gimmick is that, near the end, the audience is asked to "vote" as jurors to determine O'Neal's guilt or innocence, after watching a plot that clearly shows him innocent. After he is acquitted, a lie detector test showing the jury wrong is introduced into the film. The prosecutor, playing every string of the lurid rape theme, asks rhetorically whether we do not "love the Negro too much." Both films express clearly the undercurrent of white proletarian reservations toward the assimilation of Negroes into American life.

In the middle-brow movies of the 1960's, many New Negro social roles are depicted, usually no more than one in each film. In Hubert Cornfield's *Pressure Point,* Sidney Poitier plays a prison psychiatrist whose patient is a racial psychotic played by Bobby Darin, who is an anti-Roosevelt, anti-Semitic fascist. Thus the audience is led to accept a Negro as a doctor, if for no other reason than that the psychotic cannot. Another break from the stereotype is even more literally stated in Millard Kaufman's *Convicts Four.* The standard blues-humming Negro convict gives way to a prepossessing, aggressive convict played by Sammy Davis, who upon being assigned a new cellmate, a murderer, announces that he is not to be called "shine," that he is never to be asked to sing or dance, and finally that it is he to whom tribute is owed if the new man wishes to be protected from the hazing by the other inmates. The result is a unilateral white paper announcing that hereafter Rastus is dead. . . .

Occasionally the old stereotypes recur. In John Ford's *Man Who Shot Liberty Valence,* Woody Strode plays an Uncle Tom who shuffled off camera after being hit with a bucket of whitewash. In three Frank Sinatra comedies, Sammy Davis has played comic Negro Sambo types, especially in John Sturges' *Sergeants Three,* in which he plays Kipling's Gunga Din renamed Jonah and moved to the American frontier.

It is in the so-called art movie, independently produced on a low budget for limited distribution in small urban theaters, where one finds the most sensitive view of Negroes in American life. Artistically, this kind of film attempts to deal with reality seriously, with little concession being made to market conditions, profits, or mass taste. The first limited success of this genre was John Cassavetes' *Shadows* (1960). Using unknown actors, Ben Maddow's script attempted to show the world of Negroes as closed and esoteric by juxtaposing it with the world of whites through the medium of the anxieties of a young girl who has been passing. On the surface, it would seem that Lela Goldoni's role is simply a repeat of many other white actresses who have played Negroes, including Jeanne Crain's *Pinky*, Flora Robson in *Saratoga Trunk*, and Yvonne de Carlo in *Band of Angels.* There is not the cheap sexually charged situation of the earlier films, but only the contrast of two worlds and the need, in American society, to choose one or the other. Similar to *Shadows* was Shirley Clarke's *Cool World* which also used unknown or amateur actors and which was shot on location in Harlem from various concealed angles. The result is a fast-paced film about the habitués of the cool world of small time gangsters, junkies, and prostitutes. The movie is not a racial message or a plea to white America to send aid, but a story that uses a real part of Negro America without apology. There are sensual scenes, shots of narcotics addiction, drinking, wrecked and poor families, but the film does not piously say "look at the way these Negroes behave." It is a film about poor people who live in a city. The failure of the film, if it has one, is that few people saw it, even though in the Negro neighborhoods it was retitled *Cool World in Harlem* and luridly advertised.

The best evidence of the death of Rastus is Michael Roehmer's 1965 production, *Nothing But a Man,* the story of a marriage of a Negro railroad worker played by Ivan Dixon and a Negro school teacher played by Abbey Lincoln. They live in a small Southern town which is seen as a physical, unnamed presence pressing upon them in dozens of small ways. The pressures seem about to destroy the marriage as they destroyed the life of the railroad

From the motion picture *Nothing But a Man.* Courtesy of Audio-Brandon Films.

worker's father. The theme is not what are Negroes like, which would be a return to the stereotype, but rather, how do people behave under strain; how do they survive; how do they live as persons when the society sees them as types.

Social change has thus compelled a comparable change in some artfully made movies about Negroes; while a few other movies still deal in the old sensationalism of the contradictory stereotypes of comedy, sexuality, brutality, and laziness. Neither is the norm for American movie-going behavior. In most middle-brow films of the 1960's, Negro characters had changed into perfectly abstinent, courageous paragons of virtue as stifling and destructive of mature characterization as the old Rastus stereotype. This new unreality is evident in the absence of adult sexual behavior in the films of Sidney Poitier. In *Blackboard Jungle* women characters were carefully segregated from Poitier; in *The Defiant Ones* he is chained to a male character and confronts no women; in *Raisin in the Sun,* he is married, but residing in his mother's crowded apartment; in *Lilies of the Field* his co-stars are a gaggle of nuns; in *The Long Ships,* he is an African prince who, despite his large harem, has taken an oath of chastity. One can still wonder when a commercial film will put all the parts of *the* Negro together into a whole man.

FOR DISCUSSION

1. What is your reaction to Ossie Davis's explanation of the origins of the Stepin Fetchit image and its use during slavery as a survival tactic? Examine some of the historical literature on slavery (particularly Kenneth M. Stampp's *The Peculiar Institution*) to first see how accurate Davis's analysis is.

2. In his lengthy summary of the portrayal of the Black man on the screen until 1944, L. D. Reddick sets the tone for the standard argument that Blacks have been perennially filmed as negative stereotypes. After screening one or more of the films mentioned in his article, to what extent do you agree with his complaint? Do any of the portrayals you have witnessed deviate from Reddick's list of "standard" Negro roles?

3. Reddick details what he calls "Patterns of Change" towards the end of his article. One of these he notes (as of 1944) is "That films have improved somewhat during the present war." He is obviously referring to the heroic roles for Black actors in World War II propaganda films like *Bataan* (1943) and *Sahara* (1944). In the section by Thomas Cripps on Blacks in movies since 1945, we notice that to a certain extent these heroic images have continued in the films of Sidney Poitier. What are some of the reasons behind this shifting portrayal? Is the propaganda of the World War II films a sincere recognition of the Black man's humanity, or merely an effort to demonstrate Americans as a united front against foreign enemies? Are the post-war social dramas (however artificial these look today), like *Pinky* and *Home of the Brave,* indications that the national attitude towards the Black man had changed? What social factors could motivate such a change? Are Blacks on the screen any more human in these more complex portrayals?

4. Another of the "Patterns of Change" Reddick discusses deals with the limitations of the all-Negro film (*Hallelujah, Cabin In the Sky, Stormy Weather,* and later, *Porgy and Bess, Carmen Jones,* etc.). The author charges that these limitations are not only on the Negro but "on the development of the movie as an art form and as an organ of democratic culture." How do you feel about these all-Black films? Are they showcases for Black talent or "Jim-Crow" vehicles in which the stereotypes are confirmed? Despite Reddick's label on all-Black films as "undemocratic," could you make a case for them if they were made by Black filmmakers?

5. At the conclusion of his article, Reddick lists seven recommendations for the film industry to consider. With how many of these do you agree? Based on your reading of Thomas Cripps' article and your viewing of some recent films of this genre, how many of these recommendations have actually been implemented since 1944? What might you add to Reddick's list based on the portrayal of Black people in films today?

Note: Keep these questions in mind as you read through the specific examples of this anthology. Note the various ways writers on this subject have dealt with the themes presented by Reddick and Cripps.

PART TWO

The Birth of a Nation

As commented on in Part One, the 1915 motion picture, *The Birth of a Nation,* presented a narrow, essentially anti-Black interpretation of pre- and post-Civil War American history. Cinematically, of course, the film was an unprecedented masterpiece—a pioneer in film style and technique. This factor made its propaganda all the more devastating.

This section is devoted to understanding the impact of D. W. Griffith's film. Film historian Lewis Jacobs provides a useful outline of *The Birth of a Nation*'s plot and characters, which can be especially helpful if the film is not available for screening. The pieces following his article are reprints from the 1915, 1916, and 1965 editions of *The Crisis,* the official journal of the NAACP (edited by W. E. B. DuBois in 1915 and 1916), which convey the voice of the frustrated efforts to stop the film.

Many years after the release of *The Birth of a Nation,* the controversial debate over it continued. By the 1940's, significant film cuts were finally made prior to each of its re-releases. This time its defenders, seeing themselves as the underdogs, pleaded for the film to be shown uncut to restore its artistic framework. The final reprint is perhaps the best known and most articulate defense of the film, made by the late critic, James Agee, whose comments served as a eulogy to Griffith.

The Birth of a Nation

Lewis Jacobs

(from *The Rise of the American Film*)

The first American picture to get a two-dollar top admission, *The Birth of a Nation* enjoyed such enduring popularity that its total earnings make it one of the greatest money-makers in the history of the American screen.

The picture was first exhibited at Clune's Auditorium in Los Angeles on February 8, 1915, under the title of the book, *The Clansman.* On February 20 a print was run off in New York for the censors and a specially invited group. At this showing Thomas Dixon, the author of the original book, became so excited

From *The Rise of the American Film.* Copyright © 1937 by Harcourt Brace Jovanovich. Reprinted by permission of the author.

that during the applause he shouted to Griffith that the title *The Clansman* was too tame for so powerful a film, that it should be renamed *The Birth of a Nation.* This became the famous picture's title.

From the moment of its public opening on March 3, 1915, at the Liberty Theater in New York, *The Birth of a Nation* won phenomenal success. It was the first film to be honored by a showing at the White House. President Woodrow Wilson is said to have remarked, "It is like writing history with lightning." Critics, greeting the picture with boundless enthusiasm, called it "a new milestone in film artistry, astonishing even the most sanguine by its success, and inspiring the most dramatic new departure in dissipating the supremacy of the theater." *Variety* excitedly headlined its front page with "Griffith's $2 Feature Film Sensation of M. P. Trade," going on to say that "daily newspaper reviewers pronounced it the last word in picture making. . . . Mr. Griffith has set such a pace, it will be a long time before one will come along that can top him in point of production, action, photography, and direction," and concluding its lengthy panegyric with the pronouncement, "This picture is a great epoch in picture-making, great for the name and fame of D. W. Griffith and great for pictures."

This great picture reviewed the Civil War, the despoiling of the South, and the revival of the South's honor through the efforts of the Ku Klux Klan. After a short introduction which showed the bringing of slaves to America and summar-

From the motion picture **The Birth of a Nation.** Courtesy of Museum of Modern Art.

ized the abolitionist movement, the story proper began with Phil and Tod Stoneman, of Pennsylvania, visiting their boarding-school chums, the Cameron boys, at Piedmont, South Carolina. Phil Stoneman falls in love with Margaret Cameron, while Ben Cameron becomes enamored of the daguerreotype of Phil's sister, Elsie Stoneman. Then the Civil War breaks out. Phil and Tod leave to fight for the Union, while Ben and his two brothers join the Confederate Army. During the ensuing war years the two younger Cameron boys and Tod are killed; Piedmont undergoes "ruin, devastation, rapine and pillage." Ben, the "Little Colonel," is wounded and becomes the prisoner of Captain Phil Stoneman. Nursed by Elsie Stoneman, Ben finally recovers. Elsie and his mother visit Lincoln, "the Great Heart," and win Ben's release.

The father of Elsie and Phil Stoneman is a leader in Congress; he agitates for the punishment of the South. Lincoln refuses to countenance revenge, but Stoneman persists with his plans and grooms the mulatto, Silas Lynch, to become a "leader of his people." After the surrender at Appomattox and the assassination of Abraham Lincoln, Stoneman swiftly gains power. With Elsie and Phil he goes to the South to carry out his "equality" program for the Negroes. He rents a house next door to the Camerons'. Elsie and Ben now become engaged, but Margaret cannot bring herself to accept Phil.

Meanwhile the Reconstruction period has started.

> The reign of the carpet-baggers begins. The "Union League," so-called, wins the ensuing State election. Silas Lynch, the mulatto, is chosen Lieutenant-Governor. A legislature, with carpet-bag and Negro members in overwhelming majority, loots the state. Lawlessness runs riot. Whites are elbowed off the streets, overawed at the polls, and often despoiled of their possessions.

The organization of the "invisible empire" of Clansmen is thus inspired and justified. Ben Cameron becomes their leader, and when Stoneman learns of it he forces Elsie to break her engagement to Ben.

Events rapidly arouse the ire of the Clan and fill Ben with a desire for vengeance. The Camerons' Negro servant, Gus, becomes a militiaman and joins Lynch's mob. When Gus makes advances to Flora, Ben's younger sister, she flees from him through the woods until, in despair, she hurls herself over a cliff. There Ben discovers her, dying.

Later Dr. Cameron is arrested for harboring the Clansman. Phil, desperate on seeing to what lengths the carpetbaggers are going, helps to rescue the doctor. With Mrs. Cameron, Margaret, and the faithful servants, Phil and the doctor find refuge in a log cabin. Here they attempt to fight off an attack by the Negro militia. Meanwhile Lynch, to whom Elsie Stoneman has come pleading that he save Phil and the Camerons, demands that she marry him, and he confronts her father with the proposal.

The climax comes when the Clansmen, headed by Ben, arrive in the nick of time to mow down the Negro militia, take the Lynch mansion, free Elsie and the Stonemans, kill Gus, and save the Camerons in the cabin just as they are about to be massacred. Thus the Ku Klux Klan heroically dispenses "justice." A double honeymoon, symbolic of the reunion of North and South, concludes the story. An epilogue rejoices that peace reigns once again:

> The establishment of the South in its rightful place is the birth of a new nation. . . . The new nation, the real United States, as the years glided by, turned away forever from the blood-lust of War and anticipated with hope the world-millennium in which a brotherhood of love should bind all the nations.

"WILL THE KLAN SAVE THE DAY?"

[The following scene analysis of *The Birth of a Nation,* from Jacobs' *The Rise of American Film,* illustrates both the anti-Black theme and the very sophisticated film editing techniques used to heighten the audience's sympathy for the KKK.]

Shot No.

1107	*Full Shot*	Lynch has Elsie Stoneman alone in his office. Lynch turns to her, raises his two hands.
	Title	"See! My people fill the streets. With them I will build a black empire and you as a queen shall sit by my side."
1108	*Full Shot*	Lynch raises his arms in the air. Elsie sinks on chair. Lynch kneels, kisses the hem of her dress. She draws away in horror—rises—staggers to door, turning about. Lynch follows—sits at left. Elsie pounds on door.
1109	*Semi-Close-up*	(Circle vignette) Lynch leaning back in chair—smiles—indicates his people outside.
1110	(As 1108)	Elsie begs him—pleads with hands outstretched to let her go.
1111	(As 1109)	Lynch smiles at her.
1112	(As 1110)	Elsie turns away—screams.
1113	*Long Shot*	By the barn. Two Clansmen on horses come from right.
1114	*Fade-in*	Open country. Another Clansman dashes back.
	Title	"Summoning the Clans."
1115	*Semi-Close-Up*	Two Clansmen by the barn—one holding up the fiery cross—the other blowing a whistle.
1116	(As 1113) *Long Shot*	By the barn. They ride forward.

Shot
No.

1117	*Fade-in* (As 1114)	Open country. Clansman calling—comes forward.
1118	*Iris-in* (As 1116)	By the barn. Five more Clansmen (having heard signal) come forward from barn.
1119	*¾ Shot*	Lynch and Elsie. She rushes to window, left. Lynch after her—she pulls away—he shouts at her. Elsie sees it is no use—his people are outside.
1120	*Medium Long Shot*	Woods. Two Clansmen with a signal dash forward.
1121	(As 1119)	Lynch and Elsie. Lynch pounds his chest with fist, boastingly.
1122	*Fade-in Long Shot*	Stream of water. Two Clansmen dash up stream. Fade-out.
1123	(As 1121)	Lynch and Elsie. Lynch arrogantly points to window.
1124	*¾ Shot*	Inner room. Man and woman listening, furtively.
1125	(Back to 1123)	Lynch and Elsie. Lynch calls—Elsie is horrified.
1126	(As 1124)	Inner room. Man at door hears Lynch's call.
1127	*Semi-Close-up*	(Circle vignette) Door man—he enters Lynch's office.
1128	*¾ Shot* *Title*	Office—different angle. Man comes to Lynch. Elsie rises. "Lynch, drunk with power, orders his henchman to hurry preparations for a forced marriage."
1129	(As 1128)	Office. Man goes. Lynch turns to Elsie—her hand over her mouth, shocked.
1130	(As 1127)	(Circle vignette—door) Henchman rushes to carry out Lynch's order.
1131	(As 1126)	Inner room. Henchman calls subordinate—sends him out, right.
1132	(As 1125)	Elsie and Lynch. Elsie looks frantically about—rushes forward to door, left.
1133	*¾ Shot*	(Circle vignette—door) Elsie speeds to it.
1134	(As 1132)	Elsie and Lynch. Lynch shouts to her to come back.
1135	(As 1133)	(Circle vignette—door) Elsie tries to open door, can't, turns terrified.
1136	*Fade-in Long Shot*	Stream. A large group of Clansmen dash forward across shallow stream.
1137	(As 1134)	Elsie and Lynch. Lynch calls Elsie back.
1138	(As 1135)	(Circle vignette—door) Elsie comes forward, terrified.
1139	(As 1137)	Elsie comes forward slowly.
1140	*Long Shot*	Crossroads. Two Clansmen stop—give signal, dash on.

*Shot
No.*

1141	(As 1139)	Elsie and Lynch. Elsie pushes him away—rushes back to rear door—he after her—she escapes—comes forward around chairs—he chases her.
1142	*Fade-in Long Shot*	Army of Clansmen lined up and forming—Ben in background.
1143	*Semi-Close-up*	(Circle vignette) Ben on horse—surveys army (mask off).
1144	(As 1140)	Crossroads. Several more Clansmen come.
1145	*Fade-in Long Shot*	Field. Joining the army, Ben salutes.
1146	*Long Shot*	Silhouette of hill. Horsemen (tiny specks) riding along ridge.
1147	*Medium Long Shot*	Stream and cornfield. Two signal riders dash along.
1148	*Medium Shot*	(Moving) Two signal riders (camera on car precedes them).
1149	(As 1141)	Lynch and Elsie. Elsie rises from chair—she tries to get back.
1150	*Medium Shot*	Street outside Lynch's office. Horse and wagons come, followed by Negroes, etc. Two men on horses enter, also.
1151	(As 1141)	Lynch and Elsie. Elsie falls back in faint—Lynch supports her.
1152	*Medium Shot*	Entrance to Lynch's office. Horse and carriage stop before it—crowd around cheering.
1153	(As 1151)	Lynch, holding Elsie, hears—
1154	*¾ Shot*	A carriage. Stoneman steps out.
1155	*Medium Shot*	Stoneman goes on porch through cheering crowds.
1156	(As 1153)	Lynch and Elsie. Lynch draws Elsie closer to him.
1157	*¾ Shot*	Hall. Stoneman comes—knocks.
1158	(As 1156)	Lynch hears—turns to Elsie.
1159	(As 1157)	Stoneman is impatient—asks guard the trouble—guard doesn't know.
1160	(As 1158)	Lynch wonders what to do.
1161	(As 1159)	Hall. Stoneman impatient—paces—pounds cane—asks reason for delay.
1162	(As 1160)	Lynch and Elsie. Lynch carries Elsie forward.
1163	*¾ Shot*	Inner dining room. Lynch brings her forward (unconscious, hair streaming)—sets her in chair, left. Orderlies instructed to guard her.
1164	(As 1151)	Stoneman starts away.

*Shot
No.*

1165	(As 1163)	Inner dining room. Lynch leaves—crosses room.
1166	*¾ Shot*	Office. Lynch goes to outside door—unlocks it.
1167	(As 1161)	Hall. Stoneman hears—turns back—is admitted.
1168	(As 1166)	Office. Lynch and Stoneman come forward—Lynch apologizes—Stoneman gives him paper.
1169	*Long Shot*	Clansmen forming in field. More going—Ben waves.
1170	(As 1168)	Office. Stoneman starts back. Lynch stops him.
	Title	"I want to marry a white woman."
1171	(As 1170)	Stoneman pats him on shoulder—"Sure, go right ahead"—shakes hands—smiles.
	Title	"The Clans, being assembled in full strength, ride off on their appointed mission."
1172	*Fade-in Long Shot*	Field. Several hundred Clansmen come forward (horses rearing) to Ben, who salutes them. He rides off—motions to others—they follow with banners and fiery crosses in clouds of dust.
	Title	"And meanwhile other fates—"

From the motion picture **The Birth of a Nation.** Courtesy of Museum of Modern Art.

Fighting Race Calumny

(*The Crisis*, June 1915)

We gave last month a chronology of the fight of the National Association for the Advancement of Colored People against Tom Dixon's latest libel. This is a continuation of that narrative.

"The Birth of a Nation" is now being shown in New York, Boston, Los Angeles, San Francisco, and is booked for Chicago for the summer. In each place our branches have protested. In Los Angeles they got no results. In San Francisco a few objectionable scenes were eliminated.

In Des Moines, Iowa, the play cannot be presented because of the fact that Mr. S. Joe Brown some years ago introduced an ordinance which was passed prohibiting plays arousing race feeling.

In Ohio, Cleveland and Toledo branches and other agencies co-operating, kept out the play, "The New Governor," and think they can keep this out of the State.

The center of the fight has been Boston.

April 6:

The film interests attack THE CRISIS as an "incendiary" publication. They explain Jane Addams' criticism by declaring that she saw only half the film, which is absolutely false; and they declare that the film had the endorsement of the President of the United States, George Foster Peabody, Senator Jones of Washington and others.

April 9:

A hearing was held before Mayor Curley. Many prominent persons took part. A letter to us saying: "When the hearing was over a little bout occurred between Moorfield Storey and Griffith. It seems in the Boston papers that Griffith had promised Mr. Storey $10,000 for any Charity he would name if he could find a single incident in the play that was not historic. Mr. Storey asked Mr. Griffith if it was historic that a colored lieutenant governor had locked a white girl into a room in the Capitol and demanded a forced marriage in South Carolina? Mr. Griffith only answered, 'Come and see the play' and held out his hand to Mr. Storey. Mr. Storey drew back and said, 'No sir,' refusing to shake hands with him."

April 15:

George Foster Peabody, in a public letter, calls the film "unfair to the Negro and to the white equally and a travesty on sound peace principles." Senator Jones writes: "I never endorsed it," and continues, "the character of the second part of the play became evident before it began and I did not stay to see it." The Rector of Trinity Church, Boston, calls the film "untrue and unjust." Persons unconnected with this organization threw rotten eggs at the screen in New York City.

April 17:

A new feature is added to the film in Boston "portraying the advance of Negro life." A prominent New York lawyer informs us that this was done at the suggestion of Mr. Booker T. Washington. Colored citizens of Boston are refused tickets to the first exhibition of the film. The colored people persist in demanding tickets and eleven of them are arrested including Mr. W. M. Trotter, editor of the *Guardian,* and the Rev. Aaron Puller. All were discharged except the two mentioned.

April 19:

Great protest meeting in Faneuil Hall presided over by Frank B. Sanborn. Governor Walsh of Massachusetts promised to advocate a law which will enable such films to be suppressed.

April 20:

The state police of Massachusetts refuse to permit "The Birth of a Nation" to be exhibited on Sunday.

April 21:

The Massachusetts court orders elimination of the rape scene in the film. Large hearing before the legislature.

April 28:

Mrs. Carter H. Harrison, wife of the former mayor of Chicago denies that she ever approved the film. "It is the most awful thing I have seen. It would arouse racial feeling. I am a southerner and you naturally would expect me to oppose such pictures as this."

April 29:

Clergymen representing six Protestant denominations protest against the film.

April 30:

The secretary to the President of the United States replying to W. H. Lewis, of Boston, and to Bishop Walters, writes:

"Replying to your recent letter and enclosures, I beg to say that it is true that "The Birth of a Nation" was produced before the President and his family at the White House, but the President was entirely unaware of the character of the play before it was presented and has at no time expressed his approbation of it. Its exhibition at the White House was a courtesy extended to an old acquaintance."

A committee of the Massachusetts legislature reports a bill which is a compromise between several proposals. This bill places unlimited powers of censorship in the hands of the Mayor, the police commissioner and the chief justice of the municipal court. This bill has passed the lower House and is before the Senate.

May 2:

Mass meeting of 2,500 persons at Tremont Temple to protest against the film. Ex-President Eliot, Dr. S. M. Crothers, Dr. F. M. Rowley, Miss Adelene Moffat and Mr. Ralph Cobleigh were among the speakers. A mass meeting was also held on Boston Common. Mr. Cobleigh declared that Dixon had told him that the object of the film was the ultimate deportation of 10,000,000 Negroes from the United States, and the repeal of the war amendments. President Eliot said that this proposal was "inconceivable and monstrous" and "an abominable outrage." He continued:

"A more dangerously false doctrine taught by the play is that the Ku-Klux-Klan was on the whole a righteous and necessary society for the defence of Southern white men against black Legislatures led by Northern white men. This is the same sort of argument being used by the Germans to-day, that a contract may be destroyed as a military necessity. Undoubtedly, grievous conditions existed in the South, but they did not justify the utter lawlessness and atrocities which marked the trail of the Ku-Klux. There can be no worse teaching, no more mischievous doctrine than this, that lawlessness is justified when necessary."
May 5:

The Rev. A. W. Puller was discharged by the court while Mr. Trotter was fined for assault on a policeman, but entered an appeal. The judge blamed the ticket seller chiefly for the disturbance.

May 15. *Telegram from the Chicago Branch, N. A. A. C. P.:*

Mayor Thompson has unqualifiedly refused license to the photo-play "Birth of a Nation."

C. E. BENTLEY,
Treasurer, N. A. A. C. P.

Still Fighting the Film

(*The Crisis*, June 1916)

[After its citation of the apparent censorship victory in Boston in June of 1915, **The Crisis** remained relatively silent on the impact of **The Birth of a Nation** for the next year. (This, despite all of the NAACP's setbacks in censoring it elsewhere.) In June 1916 the following item appeared in **The Crisis**, indicating the scattered successes of Black organized protest against the film. In total, the campaign was essentially fruitless.]

The successes in two states and several cities won by the colored people against the producers of the great spectacle which seeks to defame them, is largely neutralized by the advertising which this opposition has given the film. But such incidents as this, copied from the Chicago *American* of April 24, explain how impossible it is for the branches of this Association to abandon the fight:

"Lafayette, Ind., April 23.—After witnessing the picture of 'The Birth of a Nation,' Henry Brocj, who five weeks ago came here from Kentucky, walked out on the main street of the city and fired three bullets into the body of Edward Manson, a Negro high school student, fifteen years old. The boy died to-night. There was no provocation for the tragedy and Brocj is in jail under charge of murder."

The City Council of Des Moines, Ia., after a splendid fight by the Branch, barred the production by a vote of 4 to 1 under authority of an ordinance which forbids stirring up race prejudice. The Gary Local succeeded for the second time in stopping the "Birth of a Nation" from showing; and the opposition has been as vigorous along the Rio Grande as the pursuit of Villa, and much more successful. Emory D. Williams, a member of the El Paso Branch, persuaded the management at Las Cruces, N. M., to refrain from showing the film; and the most objectionable features were eliminated when it was shown at Douglas, Ariz. Jasper B. Williams, President of the El Paso Branch, and U. S. Goen, formerly U. S. District Attorney, carried on a vigorous publicity campaign which was largely responsible for the successes. In Tacoma the film was blocked by a city ordinance won through the untiring efforts of Col. Albert E. Joab and Evan S. Stallcup, a son of the late Judge Stallcup, two distinguished white members of the National Association who are always to be found on the firing line in any struggle for human rights in the Northwest.

Regarding the question of credit for its suppression in Ohio, recently raised by the editor of the Cleveland *Gazette,* the only credit desired by the N. A. A. C. P. is that of having fought the thing consistently wherever we have a branch from the day of its first production in the United States. We only wish we could divide honors with more men like Harry C. Smith.

NAACP v. The Birth of a Nation

(*The Crisis,* February 1965)

THE STORY OF A 50-YEAR FIGHT

In February, 1915, "The Birth of a Nation," probably the most controversial and racially biased film in the history of the industry, was released. Produced by David W. Griffith, the motion picture was the industry's pioneer dramatic extravaganza and is today widely regarded as a production which initiated a new trend in film making.

As the film industry prepared to celebrate the birth of the 50-year-old film, the National Association for the Advancement of Colored People issued a

From *The Crisis,* February 1965.

call for renewal of the Association's long fight against the public showing of the picture which misrepresents Negroes. The call followed adoption of a resolution by the executive committee of the Association's New York State organization warning that re-issue of the film would be vigorously opposed in the state and urging the National Office to initiate nationwide action against public showing of the film.

Even before it was released, a vigorous campaign had been launched in California to halt its production inasmuch as it was known to be based upon Thomas Dixon's notorious anti-Negro novel, *The Clansman.* The novel, as did the film, glorified the Ku Klux Klan and vilified the role of Negroes in the Reconstruction period following the Civil War.

With the release of the film, 50 years ago this month, the National Association for the Advancement of Colored People, then only six years old, launched a nationwide campaign to expose the falsity and infamy of the story and to halt showing of the film on the ground that it distorted history and libeled the entire Negro race. In city after city, from Boston to Portland, Ore., NAACP branches mobilized community support to ban the film. The fledgling NAACP at that time consisted of a mere 6,000 members in 50 local units. But the impact of its campaign was felt across the nation.

Appeals were made to state and local censorship boards to deny permission to show the picture. Mayors and city councils were also called upon to outlaw it. In response to NAACP petitions, "The Birth of a Nation" was banned throughout Ohio by the State Board of Censors in 1915. It was banned also in Kansas. Massachusetts passed a law strengthening the Board of Censors. The Board, however, permitted showing of the film. The Tacoma, Wash., Branch succeeded in getting the City Council to pass an ordinance under provisions of which any production "which tends to incite race riots or race hatred," could be banned. A number of cities permitted showing of the film with deletion of some of the most offensive scenes.

Miss Jane Addams, head of Chicago's famed Hull House, and a founder of the NAACP, in an interview published in the old New York *Evening Post,* denounced the film as a "pernicious caricature of the Negro race. . . . It is certainly to be hoped that such a film can be suppressed. As an appeal to race prejudice, it is full of danger."

The Crisis (October 1915) expressed the hope "that such an artistic producer as Mr. Griffith may never again make the mistake of choosing an iniquitous story as a medium for his genius, or a quick method of accumulating a fortune."

In localities where the authorities refused to act against the film, the NAACP picketed the theatres which showed it. In 1921, NAACP members were arrested for picketing the Capitol Theatre in New York City, where "The Birth of a Nation" was being shown. The court offered to dismiss the charges if the pickets promised not to picket again. They declined. A higher court held that the pickets were within their rights and dismissed the case.

In a petition presented to the Mayor of Boston in 1921, Butler R. Wilson, secretary of the Boston NAACP Branch, cited the following reasons why the film should not be shown:

"Because it is a malicious misrepresentation of the colored people, depicting them as moral perverts.

"Because it glorifies the most abominable crime of the lynching of men, women and children by irresponsible mobs.

"Because it arouses sharp race antagonisms that embitter citizens against each other.

"Because it tends to a breach of the public peace."

In 1922, Arthur B. Spingarn, then chairman of the NAACP Legal Committee, together with Walter White, assistant secretary, and Herbert Seligman, director of publicity, submitted evidence at a public hearing before the New York Censorship Commission that showing of the film had caused disorder in Boston, Chicago, Philadelphia and elsewhere. The commission ordered deletion of certain objectionable scenes.

The NAACP's long fight to throttle this biased film continues although with less intensity than in the early days. In 1959 when a film distributing company was arranging to re-release the film for television showings, Roy Wilkins, NAACP executive secretary, in a letter to the president of the company, charged that the film "glorifies the Ku Klux Klan, completely distorts the role of the Negro in Reconstruction, and arouses racial hate." He urged that it not be shown on television.

As recently as 1962, John A. Morsell, assistant to the Executive Secretary, said, concerning the proposal to show "The Birth of a Nation" at the World's Fair in Seattle: "The NAACP for over 40 years opposed public exhibition of this defamatory film and we still regard it as suitable only for specialized screenings before students of cinema unlikely to be misled by its anti-Negro distortions. We urge strong representation by our Seattle branch . . . against showing of 'The Birth of a Nation' at an international event supposed to symbolize advance of civilization."

David Wark Griffith

James Agee

(*The Nation,* September 4, 1948)

He achieved what no other known man has ever achieved. To watch his work is like being witness to the beginning of melody, or the first conscious use of the lever or the wheel; the emergence, coordination, and first eloquence of language; the birth of an art: and to realize that this is all the work of one man.

We will never realize how good he really was until we have the chance to see his work as often as it deserves to be seen, to examine and enjoy it in detail as exact as his achievement. But even relying, as we mainly have to, on years-old memories, a good deal becomes clear.

One crude but unquestionable indication of his greatness was his power to create permanent images. All through his work there are images which are as impossible to forget, once you have seen them, as some of the grandest and simplest passages in music or poetry.

The most beautiful single shot I have seen in any movie is the battle charge in *The Birth of a Nation.* I have heard it praised for its realism, and that is deserved; but it is also far beyond realism. It seems to me to be a perfect realization of a collective dream of what the Civil War was like, as veterans might remember it fifty years later, or as children, fifty years later, might imagine it. I have had several clear mental images of that war, from almost as early as I can remember, and I didn't have the luck to see *The Birth of a Nation* until I was in my early twenties; but when I saw that charge, it was merely the clarification, and corroboration, of one of those visions, and took its place among them immediately without seeming to be of a different kind or order. It is the perfection that I know of, of the tragic glory that is possible, or used to be possible, in war; or in war as the best in the spirit imagines or remembers it.

This is, I realize, mainly subjective; but it suggests to me the clearest and deepest aspect of Griffith's genius: he was a great primitive poet, a man capable, as only great and primitive artists can be, of intuitively perceiving and perfecting the tremendous magical images that underlie the memory and imagination of entire peoples. If he had achieved this only once, and only for me, I could not feel that he was what I believe he is; but he created many such images, and I suspect that many people besides me have recognized them, on that deepest level that art can draw on, reach, and serve. There are many others in that one film: the homecoming of the defeated hero; the ride of the Clansmen; the rapist and his victim among the dark leaves; a glimpse of a war hospital; dead young soldiers after battle; the dark, slow movement of the Union Army away from the camera, along a valley which is quartered strongly between hill-shadow and sunlight; all these and still others have a dreamlike absoluteness which, indeed, cradles and suffuses the whole film.

This was the one time in movie history that a man of great ability worked freely, in an unspoiled medium, for an unspoiled audience, on a majestic theme which involved all that he was; and brought to it, besides his abilities as an inventor and artist, absolute passion, pity, courage, and honesty. *The Birth of a Nation* is equal with Brady's photographs, Lincoln's speeches, Whitman's war poems; for all its imperfections and absurdities it is equal, in fact, to the best work that has been done in this country. And among moving pictures it is alone, not necessarily as "the greatest"—whatever that means—but as the one great epic, tragic film.

(Today, *The Birth of a Nation* is boycotted or shown piecemeal; too many more or less well-meaning people still accuse Griffith of having made it an anti-Negro movie. At best, this is nonsense, and at worst, it is vicious nonsense. Even if it were an anti-Negro movie, a work of such quality should be shown, and shown whole. But the accusation is unjust. Griffith went to almost preposterous lengths to be fair to the Negroes as he understood them, and he understood them as a good type of Southerner does. I don't entirely agree with him; nor can I be sure that the film wouldn't cause trouble and misunderstanding, especially as advertised and exacerbated by contemporary abolitionists; but Griffith's absolute desire to be fair, and understandable, is written all over the picture; so are degrees of understanding, honesty, and compassion far beyond the capacity of his accusers. So, of course, are the salient facts of the so-called Reconstruction years.)

FOR DISCUSSION

1. In its protest over the anti-Black content of *The Birth of a Nation,* the NAACP had three basic alternatives: ignore it, urge censorship, or finance their own films as counter-propaganda. Obviously, the NAACP chose a fight for censorship, the results of which we are now aware. What about the other choices? Could Blacks have ignored the film? Is it possible that their vocal protests only drew attention to the film, thus backfiring their original purpose? Was there any possibility that Black leaders like W. E. B. DuBois, together with White NAACP colleagues, could have created and mobilized their own film company, portraying Blacks in a more favorable light? Ultimately, what impact could such a move have had on a society just awakening to the power of motion pictures?

2. In defense of *The Birth of a Nation,* James Agee, writing in the late 1940s, implied that the bulk of the content of the film is in keeping with the standard historical interpretations on the Reconstruction Period. With the exception of *Black Reconstruction,* the lengthy work of Black scholar W. E. B. DuBois (written in 1935, and generally disregarded by the

historical profession for many years, probably because DuBois was Black and a Marxist), it is true that most historians basically accepted the interpretation presented in the film ("Evil" Northern Carpetbaggers; Negro "dupes"; and poor, defenseless White Southerners). In recent years, a significant reappraisal of the Reconstruction Period has occurred, led by historians like Kenneth M. Stampp (*The Era of Reconstruction*) and Eric McKitrick (*Andrew Johnson and Reconstruction*), which disproves many of the earlier generalizations about the period. This should be kept in mind when considering the controversy over *The Birth of a Nation.* How could Black and White "liberal" organizations mount an effective protest against the film in opposition to the accepted historical interpretation of the post-Civil War era? In what ways do the standard defenses of *The Birth of a Nation* rationalize for America's anti-Black history in general?

3. Its explicit White racism to the contrary, D. W. Griffith's *The Birth of a Nation* is considered to be a cinematic masterpiece. Critic James Agee argues that the film should be appreciated as a work of art. Do you agree with this evaluation? Can a film as loaded with racist content and biased political sentiment as this one be judged solely on its artistic merit? Explain your feeling about this. (If you have seen the film, analyze your own reactions to it in this regard. Try to imagine yourself screening it in 1915 when all of its cinematic techniques were considered revolutionary innovations).

4. *The Birth of a Nation* is one of the few films where the long-existent sexual stereotype of the Black man as a bestial, oversexed creature (personified in the character of Gus, who lusts after the White heroine) was portrayed on the screen. This theme was almost never repeated in portraying Blacks in films in later years. Indeed (and you will notice this in the next two sections), Blacks have since been made to appear sexless. What do you think motivated D. W. Griffith to exploit the character of Gus? Did his characterization reinforce the attitudes of most Whites? Can you explain the toning down of *all* sexuality in Black screen roles since *The Birth of a Nation?*

PART THREE

Stepin Fetchit to Carmen Jones—
Some Samples of Opinion (1929-1955)

This section is designed to provide a sampling of the wide variety of critical opinion on the portrayal of Blacks on the screen in the three decades following *The Birth of a Nation.*

The first two pieces are reprinted from The National Urban League's magazine, *Opportunity.* Both were written in 1929 and both express a general optimism about the potential of Blacks in the movie industry. The article by the noted White humorist, Robert Benchley, on actor Stepin Fetchit, is particularly interesting (see Question 2 on p. 71.)

The optimism of these pieces, however, is ridiculed by the scathing protests of Sterling Brown (on *Imitation of Life*), and the Brooklyn Chapter of The National Negro Congress (on *Gone with the Wind*).

The all-Black film of the 1940s, *Cabin In the Sky* (which was written and produced by Whites, as were *all* of the other so-called "All Negro" films: *Hallelujah, The Green Pastures, Stormy Weather,* etc.), was generally held in high regard by White *New York Times* critic, Bosley Crowther, while condemned in the Black *New York Amsterdam News.* (Crowther's piece is interesting in its optimism about the rise of "new," more positive Black screen images during World War II.)

Two of the last essays in this section, by Black writers Ralph Ellison and James Baldwin, should serve as fitting syntheses of the problem of the stereotyping of Blacks in movies in the years after World War II.

The Negro Invades Hollywood

Floyd C. Covington

(*Opportunity,* April 1929)

What part, if any, does the Negro play in the motion picture industry of California? Behind the walls of the legion studios which festoon the Hollywood district, what place has the Negro taken in the cinematographic world? These questions are, no doubt, in the minds of the casual observers who live outside the environs of "Filmland."

Reprinted with permission of the National Urban League, Inc.

When one attempts to catalogue the information which might answer these questions he is apt to find enthusiasm more abundant than figures. However, it is apparent from observation and available statistics that Negroes have been employed in the motion picture industry in various capacities for a period of years. The major portion of these have been (and are) employed as "extras" to create atmosphere in jungle, South Sea Island and African scenes as natives, warriors, and the like. In scenes requiring domestics of color the Negro is employed to do these "bits." Others are employed to do individual roles or "parts" such as mammy types and other character sketches that receive camera close-ups and remain prominent throughout the picture. Many within this latter group are exceptionally talented, and their names are included with the other principals in the respective pictures.

In previous years the custom has been for each studio to operate its own casting office and hire those who applied at its gates for employment. In January, 1926 the fourteen leading picture corporations of California, namely, Metropolitan, United Artists, Hal Roach, Christie, F. B. O., Mack Sennett, Educational, Universal, Pathe, Warner Bros., William Fox, First National, Paramount, and Metro-Goldwyn-Mayer organized the Central Casting Corporation at Hollywood. This agency acts as a clearing house for "extras" of all types for the fourteen named studios. Approximately 11,000 adult applicants are registered according to type at the Central Casting and are available for immediate call from any of the studios.

The Casting Agency has among its personnel a Negro casting director who is one of the salaried employees of the company. The director, Mr. Chas. E. Butler, has been with the organization for about two years. He has been engaged in casting work for more than five years and was formerly with the Cinema-Auxiliary. Mr. Butler is responsible for the collecting, classifying, and distributing of the Negro "extras." His job is not an easy one. During the staging of the all-Negro talking picture "Hallelujah" he was responsible for more than 340 "extras" to report at the studio one Sunday morning. The particular scene—a camp meeting service—required types who could both sing and act. Interestingly enough, the church choirs of the city were practically empty for the day.

Those individuals who do "parts" are employed usually under contract by the individual studios. The records of these employees are not kept by the Central Casting but by the casting offices of the various companies. It is very difficult to get definite figures concerning this group as the offices are reluctant to give any information concerning salaries or length of contracts. Each company may have on their list various Negro types which are used in their pictures. On the other hand these types are interchangeable. When a picture contract expires at one studio the company releases the individual who is then free to offer his services to any other having need of his type. For example Mr. Zack Williams recently roled as "Deacon" in Fox's all-Negro talking picture "Hearts in Dixie" has been doing "parts" in pictures for the past eighteen years.

He is an unusually large physical type which enables him to enjoy quite a wide range of parts.

It is interesting to note that Negroes have been employed in large numbers in many of Lon Chaney's pictures. In "West of Zanzibar" more than one hundred were used as natives. In "Big City" eighty were used in the Harlem Nite Club scene. In the "Road to Mandalay" and "Diamond Handcuffs" more than two hundred were used as natives for atmosphere. In the latter picture one hundred men of picked physical type measuring six feet upwards were used in the Kimberly diamond mines scene. In Mr. Chaney's current picture "East is East" Negroes are being used with a few Chinese and Filipinoes as natives of Siam. Lon Chaney has been willing to demonstrate the racial versatility of the Negro by using them in his pictures for Eskimos, Chinese, Malays, Africans, and many other types of Oriental character. Mr. Locan, Mr. Chaney's assistant, stated that Negroes had been more successful doing Oriental parts than the actual racial types. He expressed the opinion that Negroes are natural actors and easier to handle before the camera. He gives Mr. Chaney's opinion in the matter by saying, "You can pull any one of them out of the mob and they can act. It is only a matter of makeup and costume to create anything from a Chinaman to an Eskimo. They require no interpreters and are always available in large numbers."

The approximate number of Negroes employed through the Central Casting is available for the years 1924 (3,464); 1925 (3,559); 1926 (6,816), and 1927 (3,754). The following table shows the number of Negroes employed through the Central Casting for the year 1928. The total amount paid in wages includes those employed by the day and receiving a standard wage of five to fifteen dollars per day. The average is $7.50 per day for "extras." The amounts

Placements of Colored People by Central Casting Corporation from January 1, 1928 to December 31, 1928.

Aggregate Month	Placements	Aggregate Wages
January	308	$ 2,906.65
February	240	2,268.38
March	773	6,690.17
April	152	1,546.78
May	212	2,075.75
June	272	2,343.27
July	1,270	11,859.38
August	278	2,915.00
September	748	5,692.50
October	4,502	34,054.38
November	882	8,188.00
December	1,279	9,162.63
	10,916	$89,702.89

given in the table do not include the number of Negroes employed under contract or the amount of money paid to them. In general the wage scale of the contract group ranges from $25.00 per day to $300.00 per week and above. Perhaps the largest salaries paid to Negroes in the industry were those paid to the principals of the two all-Negro talking pictures, "Hearts in Dixie" produced by William Fox Company and "Hallelujah" by the Metro-Goldwyn-Mayer Company. The salaries in some instances approximated $1,250 per week and above. If the total amount paid to those working under contract in the above pictures and those in which Negroes have figured prominently, prior to this date, could be added to the total in the table it would be even more striking.

No charge is made by the Central Casting for the individuals whom it places through its offices. In fact the Agency makes every effort to prevent exploitation of the workers in the industry. Its attempts have gone far to reduce the number of sporadic organizations which rear their heads from time to time supposedly to make "everyone's face their fortune." The Casting is anxious that everyone should know that no worker—colored or white—has to pay for the employment which they receive in the motion picture industry.

The total number of placements for 1927 was 3,754. The total amount paid in wages for that year was $30,036. The increase in the number of Negroes used and the wages received by them is striking in comparison. Nineteen hundred twenty-eight shows an approximate increase in placement of 345 per cent; and an increase of 335 per cent in wages received.

According to Mr. Butler, the Negro "extra" receives more money than any other "extra" in the industry except Chinese. In other words, they are next to the highest paid in the industry. It must be remembered that the number of placements for the month do not represent that number of different individuals. The motion picture industry is, as far as "extras" are concerned, a seasonal industry. Some individuals may be used dozens of times within the month depending upon the various needs of the companies. Those individuals who are temporarily employed or who may leave their jobs at will are the ones who enjoy a monopoly of the industry.

The question has been continually raised whether there has been or will be a Negro star in Hollywood. The first part of the question may be disposed of by saying that there has been no Negro star to date. There have been many outstanding Negroes in pictures, but none rated as stars. The reason for that is obvious. Negroes have been employed principally for *atmosphere* in large numbers and disposed of chiefly *en masse.* Those who have reached places of importance are those who by sheer force of ability or because of the value of their distinctive type have outstripped their fellows. James B. Lowe of *Uncle Tom's Cabin* and Lincoln Peary known as *Stepin Fetchit* have reached places of importance and have, no doubt, a great future in pictures. Such names as Mattie Peters, Madam Sultewan, Gertrude Howard, George Reed, Louise Beavers, Oscar Smith, Mildred Washington, Clif Ingram, Noble Johnson, Jim Blackwell and many others have gained places of importance and have a long standing record of merit around the studios. We have already cited the distinctive work of Zack Williams.

With the introduction and improvement of talking pictures, comes, perhaps the Negro's real opportunity to produce stars in his own right. That opportunity will largely depend upon the work of such artists as Mr. Clarence Muse taking the role of "Nappus" in the Fox production "Hearts in Dixie"; and the work of Mr. Daniel Haynes and Miss Nina Mae McKenny in the Metro-Goldwyn-Mayer production of "Hallelujah." King Vidor, famous director of the "Big Parade," who is responsible for the all-Negro picture "Hallelujah" ventures an opinion: "It will either be one of the greatest successes in pictures or one of the greatest flops. Frankly, I don't know which—but believe that when colored drama succeeds as it does on the stage, it must also be good for the screen. At any rate it has injected some new ideas into pictures. . . . The Negro is one of the greatest actors by nature principally because he really doesn't act at all, but actually feels and experiences the emotions he seeks to portray."

The director, author, and assistants of the Fox picure "Hearts in Dixie" are also counting the pulse beats of the Negro's dramatic possibilities. Mr. Walter Weems, author of the scenario, and Mr. Paul Sloane, director, are exceedingly enthusiastic over the group with whom they have worked. They expressed the opinion that in all their experience in pictures they have never worked with a finer group of people—colored or white. They believe that such a group has unlimited possibilities for all phases of motion picture work.

Apparently, then, with the current venture of all-Negro talking pictures, the Negro emerges from a somewhat obscure place in the industry to take a place in the centre of the stage. It is hoped that with the increase of all-Negro pictures that the Negro will also develop directors and technicians that may aid in a large way to improve the technique of the pictures being staged around them. The time is ripe for Negro scenarists to produce stories from the rich fields—still virgin—of their folk-life. It is interesting to note here that at the M-G-M studio a young Negro who has been formerly employed as shoe shiner around the studio has made quite a rapid stride. Known as "Slickem" on the lot because of his ability to give a brilliant shine, Harold Garrison is now acting in the capacity of second assistant to King Vidor in the production of "Hallelujah."

The Negro's place in the motion picture industry in California depends largely upon himself. The future is provocative of greater possibilities. A Culver City writer expresses a view somewhat naively, "It's the day of the dark star in Hollywood . . . Perhaps there will be more Negro pictures—perhaps there will be many colored stars in the future. No one can tell yet. But the colored troupe isn't worrying much about this. They want to tell their story—the story of their race—just this once."

In the wake of this new experiment in all Negro pictures comes the Negro's chance to be articulate in his own behalf. Greater still, the success of these pictures shall erect the foundation of the Negro's permanent place in the cinematographic industry in California.

Hearts in Dixie
(The First Real Talking Picture)

Robert Benchley

(*Opportunity*, April 1929)

Ever since the inception of the talking-movie there has been a perfectly justifiable suspicion that it wouldn't work. There could be no doubt that sound could be made to come from some part of a screen on which figures were shown, sound which could be construed by eager and imaginative members of the audience to be coming from the mouths of the characters. But as for any illusion of speakers, that was more or less of a gamble.

One of the chief obstacles in the advance of the "talkies" has been the voices of the actors. Even granted that the sound could be made to come from somewhere near their mouths, the voice itself was impossible. They have either sounded like the announcer in a railway station or some lisping dancing-master, and the general effect has been to cause the public mind to revert to the good old movie days when sub-titles were flashed on and the hero and heroine were not expected to give themselves away by talking.

With the opening of "Hearts in Dixie," however, the future of the talking movie has taken on a rosier hue. Voices *can* be found which will register perfectly. Personalities *can* be found which are ideal for this medium. It may be that the talking-movies must be participated in exclusively by Negroes, but, if so, then so be it. In the Negro the sound-picture has found its ideal protagonist.

With the exception of one character (easily the worst actor in the picture) the entire cast of "Hearts in Dixie" is colored. And people who have never been able to see anything at all in the "talkies" are convinced after seeing this one. There is a quality in the Negro voice, an ease in its delivery and a sense of timing in reading the lines which make it the ideal medium for the talking-picture. What white actors are going to do to compete with it is their business. So long as there are enough Negroes to make pictures, and enough good stories for them to act in, the future of the talking-picture is assured.

The story of "Hearts in Dixie" is practically negligible. It is almost embarrassingly meagre. There are scenes on a cotton plantation, with an occasional close-up of an old man, his daughter and his grandchild in a casual family relationship. The mother dies; the child is left to the grandfather, and, as the picture ends, we see the little boy leaving on the "Nellie Blye" to go up the river to school, with the grandfather waving "goodbye" as the boat toots its way up the river. There are times in the story when you are not sure that this *is* the story, when you wonder if there is a story after all. But there are never times when you care much, for you can hear the rich resonance of the voices and

From the motion picture *Hearts in Dixie*. Courtesy of Films Inc.—20th Century Fox.

watch the unparalleled ease and grace of acting of the characters, and nothing else much matters.

Of course, entirely outside the main story (what there is of it) is the amazing personality of Stepin Fetchit. I see no reason for even hesitating in saying that he is the best actor that the talking movies have produced. His voice, his manner, his timing, everything that he does, is as near to perfection as one could hope to get in an essentially phony medium such as this. You forget that you are listening to a synchronized sound-track which winds its way along the side of a photographic film. You forget that back of all this are weeks and weeks of dull, repetitious rehearsals and stupid bickerings in the office of the producing company. When Stepin Fetchit speaks, you are there beside him, one of the great comedians of the screen.

I happen to have been in Hollywood when "Hearts in Dixie" was being made. I know that it could have been twice as good a picture as it is. I happen to know that Sloan, the director, is now in a sanitarium recovering from a nervous breakdown because his picture was tinkered with and cut to pieces to make a Jewish holiday. "Hearts in Dixie," as originally made, was a great epic of the Southern Negro. To see the little snatches of it which have been left, snatches which only suggest the wild, elemental abandon of the original, is to realize why the movies can never be an artistic source in the community so long as they are in the hands of the present group of financiers. But, even as it stands, "Hearts in Dixie" is something worth seeing, because of the actors and the direction of the actors and the inevitable feeling that the moving picture can be made to talk with some degree of illusion.

In only one respect (aside from the direction of Mr. Sloan) has the interference of the white man been beneficial. This is in the comedy dialogue. For some reasons best known to Negroes themselves, when they are left alone to write their own comedy lines, they desert their native wit and mess around with what they seem to feel white folks *want* them to say. With the exception of "Blackbirds" there has not been a Negro show in which the comedy lines have not been execrable. They usually consist of the mispronunciation of big words, and such mispronunciation as even the most ignorant of Negroes could not possibly make. To this is added the inevitable fright which a Negro is supposed to fall into when confronted by ghosts, loud noises and razors. This usually makes up the list of Negro comedy in the revues which they themselves have fashioned, and it is the most unfair of all the libels which the Negro creates against his race. For the real Negro comedy is as easy and unforced as that of Will Rogers (when his *is* unforced) and, if it could be written into a revue would easily be the most spontaneous of all American comic dialogue.

It is this heavy-handed childishness which the dialogue-writers in "Hearts in Dixie" have avoided. The lines are funny and they sound genuine, but they are not based on mispronunciation. One of the funniest comedy scenes on any screen comes in "Hearts in Dixie" when Mr. Fetchit, after as arduous a courtship as his lack of energy would allow him to make, ends by asking the lady of his choice if she loves him. And when she admits that she has been won over by his charm and does love him he says: "Then get me some more of those spare-ribs." It is all as effortless as Mr. Fetchit's comedy itself and the white dialogue writers on Mr. Fox's lot have given the Negroes a better break than they have given themselves in the past.

The fact remains, however, that many people will remember "Hearts in Dixie" as the first talking picture in which the characters seemed really to talk, and will remember its Negro cast as the first real actors they ever saw in talking-pictures.

Imitation of Life: Once a Pancake

Sterling A. Brown

(*Opportunity,* March 1935)

Imitation of Life, by Fannie Hurst, first appeared as *Sugar House* in *The Pictorial Review.* It was another American success story. Bea Pullman, a hard working, motherless girl, with a paralyzed father, forges her way, after her husband is killed in a railroad accident, from drab poverty, to Duncan Phyfe, Heppelwhite and Sheraton prosperity. She is grateful to life for her talent to "provide people with a few moments of creature enjoyment" in the shape of succulent waffles and maple syrup; she should be grateful to Delilah, upon whose broad shoulders she rode pickaback to affluence. Delilah, whose recipe and skill are the makings of the world famous enterprise, wants little but the chance, since she is full of "a rambunctious capacity for devotion," to be mammy to the whole world, and especially to Miss Bea. Her greatest trouble is her fair daughter Peola, who wants to be white in the worst way, and finally marries a young blond engineer, who, coincidentally, was never to know that he had called his mother-in-law "mammy" over a stack of wheats. Peola and husband disappear into Bolivia; Delilah obligingly dies after the business is established and Miss Bea, free at last for love, finds that it is too late, that her beloved has been swept away by her daughter, Jessie. It is, in the main, a tearful story.

Those who have seen the picture will recognize the differences in plot. The characterization and ideas, however, are little changed. Delilah, "vast monument of a woman," "her huge smile the glowing heart of a furnace," "her round black moon face shining above an Alps of bosom" is essentially the same, with her passion for rubbing "dem white little dead beat feet," the inebriation of her language, too designedly picturesque, her unintelligible character, now infantile, now mature, now cataloguing folk-beliefs of the Southern Negro, and now cracking contemporary witticisms. Her baby talk to the white child partakes too much of maple sugar; to her own, too much of mustard. Delilah's visions of going to glory recur in the book. To the reviewer they are not true folk-eloquence. "I'm paying lodge-dues an' I'm savin' mah own pennies for to be sent home and delivered to de glory of de Lawd wid plumes and trumpets blowin' louder dan rhubarb would make growin'." There is a great deal of talk on the text: "Never the Twain Shall Meet." Delilah is completely black, and therefore contented: "Lovers of de Lawd an' willin' servers is my race, filled with de blessings of humility" ... "Glory be to Gawd, I's glad I's one of his black chillun, 'cause, sho' as heaven, his heart will bleed fust wid pity and wid mercy for his lowdown ones." Peola, near white, but with "not a half moon to her finger nails" is unhappy. *"It's de white horses dat's wild, a'swimmin' in de blood of mah chile. . . . I wants to drown dem white horses plungin' in mah baby's blood."* Can one reader be forgiven, if during such passages, there runs into his mind something unmistakably like a wild horse laugh?

Remembering the book I was unprepared to believe the theatregoers and critics who urged the novelty, the breaking away from old patterns of the picture. Of course they had reasons. It is true that the picture is a departure from Stepin Fetchit. There is less of Octavus Roy Cohen in the film than in the book (perhaps the intrinsic dignity of Louise Beavers kept down the clowning.) The bandana has been exchanged for a white chef's cap. There is a warm mutual affection between the two mothers; kindheartedness meets up with gratitude. Important roles, of some seriousness, were given to Louise Beavers and Fredi Washington, who are certainly deserving actresses. If their names on the screen were not quite in the largest type, they were still high up on the list, and will be remembered because of first rate performances. Moreover, Delilah is a preternaturally good woman, except for a little breadth of diction, and Peola's morality, in spite of her bitterness, is unimpeachable. Cabins and cottonfields are a long way from the suite (downstairs) of Delilah. Both Delilah and Peola can dress up, after a fashion. Poverty is back in the past, due to Miss Bea's midas-like touch (?) and her generosity (!) "Ain't you made life a white padded cell for Delilah?" The word "nigger" is not once used, even in places where logically it should occur. Minor problems are touched upon. All of these things are undoubtedly gladdening to our bourgeois hearts. But that doesn't make them new. However novel in Hollywood, they are old in literature. It requires no searching analysis to see in *Imitation of Life* the old stereotype of the contented Mammy, and the tragic mulatto; and the ancient ideas about the mixture of the races.

Delilah is straight out of Southern fiction. Less abject than in the novel, she is still more concerned with the white Jessie than with Peola. She has little faith in Peola's capacities: "We all starts out smart; we don't get dumb till later on." Resignation to injustice is her creed; God knows best, we can't be telling Him his business; mixed bloods who want to be white must learn to take it, must not beat their fists against life; she doesn't rightly know where the blame lies. When she refuses her twenty per cent (not because it was too little) she is the old slave refusing freedom: "My own house? You gonna send me away? Don't do that to me. How I gonna take care of you and Miss Jessie if I's away? I's yo' cook. You kin have it; I make you a present of it." She finally consents for some money to be put aside against a funeral. *"Once a pancake, always a pancake."* The "passing" episodes are as unbelievable. She is ignorant of the school attended by her daughter (in Atlantic City of segregated schools); she naively gives Peola away, insisting that she did not intend to. Later, finding her daughter passing as a cashier she announces, "I'se yo' mammy, Peola," although she could have spared the girl embarrassment by sending in Miss Bea. She is canny about the ways of men and women where Miss Bea is concerned; but when her daughter is yearning for music and parties, she says, "Come on, honey, I'll dance with you." The director would not even let Delilah die in peace. She must speak, in a tragic scene, well acted, comic lines about "colored folks' eyes bulging out," and "not liking the smell of gasoline." Her idiom is good only in spots; I have heard dialect all my life, but I have yet to hear such a line as "She am an angel."

Peola, wistfully hearing the music upstairs, searching the mirror for proof of her whiteness, crying out her hatred of life, her vexation at her black mother, is the tragic octoroon, familiar to novels more than to life. She, too, is at times hard to believe in. For she never quite gets a grasp on the true problem. There was a chance for real bitterness when Miss Bea stops her as she is finally leaving her mother. But the tirade does not come, although Peola must have seen through the condescension and the gentle exploitation. It would be refreshing to have heard what a girl like Peola would really have said; I believe Miss Washington could have risen to heights in its delivery. There is a scene where Miss Bea goes upstairs while Delilah goes down. It is symbolic of many things. One is, that in *Imitation of Life* where Claudette Colbert has a role to bring out all that there is in her, both Miss Beavers and Miss Washington have, so to speak, to go downstairs; Miss Beavers to a much greater childishness, and Miss Washington to a much greater bewilderment than they would recognize in real life. But so Hollywood would have it; and so Hollywood gets something less artistic and less true.

To the reviewer the shots nearest to truth are the Harlem funeral scenes; the most memorable is the flash of the electric sign after the death of Delilah. The good old heart-broken soul dies, having made Miss Bea's road an easy one, for little more return than comfort and affection; Miss Bea goes on to wealth, love, and happiness, and Delilah gets her dubious immortality as an electrified trademark. The music of the quartette is stirring, although it is unfortunately synchronized with Delilah's dying, and is another instance of Hollywood's poor imitation of life. One of the worst shots is the renunciation finale in the romantic garden, with the lights on the river reminiscent of Venice.

It goes without saying that the picture has its moments of truth to American life. It is true, for instance, that in such a partnership, the white member, whose contributions were mild flirtations for business support, and energy, and "brains," would give the real power behind the enterprise a paltry twenty per cent. It is true that the white partner would most likely live upstairs, the black down; and that they would not ride side by side in the same automobile. It is true that after the death of the dearly beloved Mammy, the lost daughter, finding her friends again, would be gently comforted, and placed in the family car up front with the chauffeur. And it is true that for Jessie, business success would mean horse-shows, Switzerland, and finishing schools, where she could learn to stretch her eyes and simper, whereas for Peola it would mean a precarious future, remorse-ridden and threatening. All of this is true to the ways of America. But it hardly seems anything to cheer about.

The Littlest Rebel

(*Variety*, December 25, 1935)

[This is a contemporary review of a standard 1930s musical comedy, *The Littlest Rebel,* with Shirley Temple. This film made wide use of stereotyped portrayals of Blacks and was generally applauded in the White press as "charming."]

20th Century-Fox release of B. G. DeSylva production. Stars Shirley Temple. Features John Boles, Jack Holt, Karen Morley, Bill Robinson. Directed by David Butler. Screen story by Edwin Burke based on Edward Peble play. Camera, John Seitz; sound, S. C. Chapman. At Radio City Music Hall, N. Y., week Dec. 19, '35. Reunning time, 73 mins.

Virgie Cary	Shirley Temple
Capt. Herbert Cary	John Boles
Col. Morrison	Jack Holt
Mrs. Cary	Karen Morley
Uncle Billy	Bill Robinson
Sergeant Dudley	Guinn Williams
James Henry	Willie Best
Abraham Lincoln	Frank McGlynn, Sr.
Mammy	Bessie Lyle
Sally Ann	Hannah Washington

"The Littlest Rebel" is a good Shirley Temple picture. Which means money. It happens to be very similar in title, plantation locale, Negro comedy, and in general mechanics to "The Little Colonel." Probably that won't dampen the enthusiasm of the Temple worshippers. All the youngster's pictures follow a pattern and in this instance producer DeSylva and director Butler have put on a particularly smooth lacquer with several standout sequences.

Shrewdly playing both sides, as between the north and the south, Edwin Burke's script throws a lot of dialog to the Confederacy. Without actually saying so the lines imply things that will make the South purr with pride. One line about "the man up north that wanted to free the slaves" is spotted and delivered by Bill Robinson in such a way as to possibly cause northern eyebrows to tilt. Just a slight tilt. But the picture winds up with a touching scene in the White House with Shirley Temple seated on Lincoln's lap and divvying an apple, piece for piece, with the President.

All bitterness and cruelty has been rigorously cut out and the Civil War emerges as a misunderstanding among kindly gentlemen with eminently happy slaves and a cute little girl who sings and dances through the story.

Bill Robinson and the child again dance. This is surefire, and it bespeaks plenty of hoofing rehearsal. Robinson is once more the trusty family butler who guards little missy. No trace of the Edward Peple play in the Burke film version. As a play "The Littlest Rebel" introduced Mary Miles Minter, then a child actress, to the legit stage.

From the motion picture *The Littlest Rebel.* Courtesy of Films Inc.—20th Century Fox.

John Boles, Jack Holt and Karen Morley are just routine adults who react to the charm of a little girl. Acting honors belong to Shirley Temple, Bill Robinson, Frank McGlynn, Sr., as Lincoln, and Willie Best, a droll Negro nitwit.

Picture opens just before war is declared. The tot is giving a party to all the well mannered children of the Virginia aristocracy and a good deal of sly comedy is slipped in at the table, and later when the children skip the minuet with genteel dignity. War brings successive losses culminating in the death of the mother (Karen Morley). Story is synthetic throughout but smart showmanship instills the illusion of life. Besides which the picture has good tempo.

Lies About Lincoln, American Democracy, and Negro People!

Brooklyn Chapter, National Negro Congress
(A Broadside on *Gone with the Wind*, 1939)

Just as in the book, the film "Gone with the Wind" in an insidious way is one of the most vicious assaults upon the treasured liberties and democratic principles which the American people won during Lincoln's time. The "sectionalism" which was one of the causes championed by the slave-masters and finally involved America into four years of Civil War, is openly justified in the film and fanned again into flames of race-baiting Negro prejudice. "Why doesn't the North let us secede in peace?" one bourbon in the picture says in a clever attempt to place responsibility for the war on those who wanted human liberty.

The Negro people are vilified in a shameful fashion and portrayed as so many subservient, content and willing slaves who would literally lay down their lives for their masters, because they enjoy and appreciate chattel slavery. According to this picture, the Negro people did not want freedom, they wanted to remain slaves. They are pictured along with Union soldiers and carpetbaggers in such scenes as to justify the Ku Klux Klan.

America's glorious history is deliberately distorted. The Civil War and especially the Reconstruction Era is turned upside down so as to please only those who love slavery. The Union Army of Emancipation is slandered as one of destruction, murder, rapine, terror and plunder. It is pictured as responsible for the burning of Atlanta, with the pillaging and the plundering of everything and everyone in sight; when it is an historical truth that these were the evil doings of the retreating Confederate forces. The Union veterans of the Civil War, better known as the G.A.R. (Grand Army of the Republic), have already voted to boycott the picture because "Gone with the Wind" is a travesty on our democracy and that great humanitarian, Abraham Lincoln.

One of the most glorious periods in American History was the Reconstruction Era. In fact, it is the only time that there has been any semblance of democracy in the South. Negro Senators, Congressmen and State Legislators sat together and shared equally with their white brothers the responsibilities of administering good government, quite unlike its "Tobacco Road" of today, and its disfranchisement of more than 75% of the Negro and white population.

We feel that "Gone with the Wind" is a disgrace to our country and its institutions. We applaud the action of the G.A.R. and are confident that the , people of Brooklyn will receive the opening of "Gone with the Wind" at the Loew's Metropolitan Theatre, Thursday evening, February 1, with similar condemnation.

"Cabin" Picture Called Insult

Ramona Lewis

(New York Amsterdam News, June 12, 1943)

The celluloid version of "Cabin in the Sky" goes into its second week at the Criterion on Broadway. In spite of this magnificent cast, this first all Negro picture to be made by MGM since "Hallelujah" is an insult masking behind the label of folklore. It isn't folklore.

Go to the library and do a little research on your own and you will find that Negro folklore is of different stuff. And it's an insult because it pictures Negroes, heads tied up, with crap shooting inclinations and prayer meeting propensities at a time when Negroes are daily proving their heroic mettle in battle and defense plant. This is the sort of thing that keeps alive misconceptions of the Negro.

The picture which was opened in New York with some trepidation lest it offend the eyes of the wary has been breaking all house records at the Criterion. Since box office returns convince Hollywood more than anything else that it is in the right, it's too bad the actors didn't have the courage to refuse to make the film in the first place.

The Story's Cast

The story as you probably know concerns the struggle of Lucifer, Jr. and a general of the Lord for the soul of Little Joe. Lucifer nearly wins out, but the praying of Petunia, Little Joe's wife, saves the day. Judging from the patronizing sounds emitted by the whites sitting around this reviewer, the audience seemed to believe this was the normal pattern of Negro life.

Ethel Waters remains in her original role as Petunia and Rex Ingram is still the irresistible Lucifer, Jr. The beautiful Lena Horne does Georgia Brown, the part Katherine Dunham played on the stage; Rochester is Little Joe, the role Dooley Wilson created, and Kenneth Spencer is the dignified general of the Lord.

This review by Ms. Lewis appeared originally in the *New York Amsterdam News,* June 12, 1943.

Cleaving the Color Line

Bosley Crowther

(*The New York Times,* June 6, 1943)

For a long time a great many people have been rightfully distressed—not to say indignant and outraged—at the treatment the Negro generally receives in films. With good and sufficient reason, these persons have stoutly maintained that the usual Hollywood concept of the Negro constitutes a grave social abuse and that the tolerance of the color line in pictures is one of the bulwarks of that cruel stigma today. Naturally, such persons bridle when a Negro is shown on the screen as a bowing and scraping menial of the old "yassa, Massa" stripe or a "kyaw-kyawing" Sambo designed mainly to tickle the white folks with his japes. And so they have bridled often, for most of the Negroes in films have been one or the other type.

Of late, though, a certain realization of racial equity has run through Hollywood, mainly because attention has been directed thereto by influential persons and groups. And a few rather striking indications of sensibility have been notable in recent films. The character Sam in "Casablanca," which Dooley Wilson so touchingly played, was a remarkable break from the traditional ranking of black and white on separate social planes. (As a matter of fact, Warner Brothers, the studio that made the film, has generally had a more liberal and realistic appreciation of Negroes. Its frank presentation of the dilemma of a young Negro in "In This Our Life" was one of the few genuine features of an otherwise trashy film.) The respectful conception of a black man, played by Leigh Whipper, in "The Ox-Bow Incident" is one of the many distinctions of that grimly realistic film. And the Negro soldier played by Kenneth Spencer in the new war film, "Bataan," is a fine, dignified notation of the share of his race in the war. (We blush to mention the clumsy and patronizing way that Twentieth Century-Fox dragged a grinning Jazzbo into its submarine picture, "Crash Dive.")

Fancy Free

Slowly some steps are being taken to give the Negro his due on the screen—perhaps no more forward than backward, but at least some respectable steps. And, as a consequence, this writer sees no reason for laboring an anti-racial point (as some have done) in connection with such a charming and melodious all-Negro musical fantasy as "Cabin in the Sky." This new and delightful Metro picture, now showing at Loew's Criterion, is frankly a figment of the fancy, no more pretentious of reality than was "The Green Pastures." It is carefully placed, by its preface, in the category of legend or tall-tale and, far from belittling Negroes, it treats them with affectionate respect.

The story is that of Petunia Jackson and her ever-loving husband, Little Joe, who has occasional soft leanings toward one Georgia Brown and the galloping dominoes. Well, at a most unfortunate moment, Little Joe suffers critical wounds and, while he teeters at death's door, the son of the devil and a soldier of the Lord vie for his soul. They decide to give Little Joe one more chance—restore him to health with a six-month reprieve, during which he will show by his actions whether he goes up above or down below. And the rest of the story is concerned with the immortal struggle for Little Joe, with the soldier of the Lord working through Petunia, a faithful servant, and Lucifer Jr. working through the sleek Miss Brown.

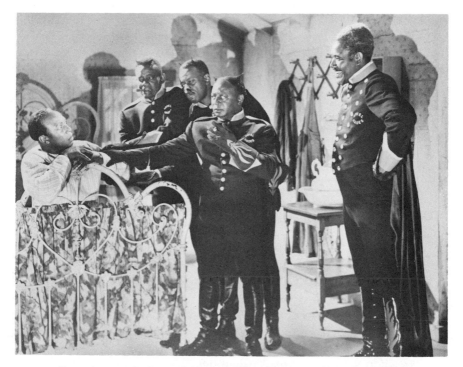

From the motion picture *Cabin in the Sky.* Courtesy of Films Inc.—MGM.

No Offense

It is one of those uncommon pictures which bursts with vitality—and that in itself is a tribute to the Negro performers in it, for certainly the run of musicals with white actors has been hackneyed and dull. Ethel Waters is grand as Petunia. When she puts the power or pathos of her voice into the singing of such memorable numbers from the original stage show as the title song or "Taking a Chance on Love," or into a haunting new torch song called "Happiness Is Just a Thing Called Joe," she makes your flesh tingle and your eyes mist. Miss Waters can sing a song. And Eddie (Rochester) Anderson is really cute as Little Joe—maybe not as truly affecting as was Dooley Wilson in the original, but pleasantly brisk and rapscallionly, with gentleness and kindness underneath. Lena Horne is gaudy as Georgia and sings a couple of numbers neatly; Rex Ingram and Kenneth Spencer are formidable as the rival fates and a whole slue of swell Negro performers—all good "names"—fill out other roles.

True, the conception of the Negro is sentimental in "Cabin in the Sky." It is also blurred with the usual complacency toward the Negro's lot. The hero is an always-lovable "no 'count," his wife sings joyously over her tubs. They live in a shack and are contented. All of them are superstitious and illiterate. That is a complacent picture. No denying it. But, within the recognized scope of musical fantasy, it certainly cannot be condemned of violating fact and it makes for some lively entertainment. Heaven knows, there have been enough "white" musicals which have been much more careless of realities and much less delightful to see.

The Shadow and the Act

Ralph Ellison

(*The Reporter,* December 6, 1949)

Faulkner has given us a metaphor. When, in the film *Intruder in the Dust,* the young Mississipian Chick Mallison falls into an ice-coated creek on a Negro's farm, he finds that he has plunged into the depth of a reality which constantly reveals itself as the reverse of what it had appeared before his plunge. Here the ice—white, brittle and eggshell-thin—symbolizes Chick's inherited views of the world, especially his Southern conception of Negroes. Emerging more shocked by the air than by the water, he finds himself locked in a moral struggle with the owner of the land, Lucas Beauchamp, the son of a slave, who, while aiding the boy, angers him by refusing to act toward him as Southern Negroes are expected to act.

To Lucas, Chick is not only a child but his guest. Thus he not only dries the boy's clothes, he insists that he eat the only food in the house, Lucas's own dinner. When Chick (whose white standards won't allow him to accept the hospitality of a Negro) attempts to pay him, Lucas refuses to accept the money. What follows is one of the most sharply amusing studies of Southern racial ethics to be seen anywhere. Asserting his whiteness, Chick throws the money on the floor, ordering Lucas to pick it up; Lucas, disdaining to quarrel with a child, has Chick's young Negro companion, Aleck Sander, return the coins.

Defeated but still determined, Chick later seeks to discharge his debt by sending Lucas and his wife a gift. Lucas replies by sending Chick a gallon of molasses by—outrage of all Southern Negro outrages!—a white boy on a mule. He is too much, and from that moment it becomes Chick's passion to repay his debt and to see Lucas for once "act like a nigger." The opportunity has come, he thinks, when Lucas is charged with shooting a white man in the back. But instead of humbling himself, Lucas (from his cell) tells, almost orders, Chick to prove him innocent by violating the white man's grave.

In the end we see Chick recognizing Lucas as the representative of those virtues of courage, pride, independence and patience that are usually attributed only to white men—and, in his uncle's words, accepting the Negro as "the keeper of our [the whites'] consciences." This bit of dialogue, coming after the real murderer is revealed as the slain man's own brother, is, when viewed historically, about the most remarkable concerning a Negro ever to come out of Hollywood.

With this conversation, the falling into creeks, the digging up of corpses and the confronting of lynch mobs that mark the plot, all take on a new significance: Not only have we been watching the consciousness of a young Southerner grow through the stages of a superb mystery drama, we have participated in a process by which the role of Negroes in American life has been given what, for the movies, is a startling new definition.

To appreciate fully the significance of *Intruder in the Dust* in the history of Hollywood we must go back to the film that is regarded as the archetype of the modern American motion picture, *The Birth of a Nation.*

Originally entitled *The Clansman,* the film was inspired by another Southern novel, the Reverend Thomas Dixon's work of that title, which also inspired Joseph Simmons to found the Knights of the Ku Klux Klan. (What a role these malignant clergymen have played in our lives!) Re-entitled *The Birth of a Nation* as an afterthought, it was this film that forged the twin screen image of the Negro as bestial rapist and grinning, eye-rolling clown—stereotypes that are still with us today. Released during 1915, it resulted in controversy, riots, heavy profits and the growth of the Klan. Of it Terry Ramsaye, a historian of the American motion-picture industry writes: "The picture . . . and the K.K.K. secret society, which was the afterbirth of a nation, were sprouted from the same root. In subsequent years they reacted upon each other to the large profit of both. The film presented predigested dramatic experience and thrills. The society made the customers all actors in costume."

Usually *The Birth of a Nation* is discussed in terms of its contributions to cinema technique, but, as with every other technical advance since the oceanic sailing ship, it became a further instrument in the dehumanization of the Negro. And while few films have gone so far in projecting Negroes in a malignant light, few before the 1940s showed any concern with depicting their humanity. Just the opposite. In the struggle against Negro freedom, motion pictures have been one of the strongest instruments for justifying some white Americans' anti-Negro attitudes and practices. Thus the South, through D. W. Griffith's genius,

From the motion picture *Intruder in the Dust.* Courtesy of Films Inc.—MGM.

captured the enormous myth-making potential of the film form almost from the beginning. While the Negro stereotypes by no means made all white men Klansmen, the cinema did to the extent that audiences accepted its image of Negroes, make them participants in the South's racial ritual of keeping the Negro "in his place."

After Reconstruction the political question of what was to be done with Negroes, "solved" by the Hayes-Tilden deal of 1876, came down to the psychological question: "How can the Negro's humanity be evaded?" The problem, arising in a democracy that holds all men as created equal, was a highly moral one: democratic ideals had to be squared with anti-Negro practices. One answer was to *deny* the Negro's humanity—a pattern set long before 1915. But with the release of *The Birth of a Nation* the propagation of subhuman images of Negroes became financially and dramatically profitable. The Negro as scapegoat could be sold as entertainment, could even be exported. If the film became the main manipulator of the American dream, for Negroes that dream contained a strong dose of such stuff as nightmares are made of.

We are recalling all this not so much as a means of indicting Hollywood as by way of placing *Intruder in the Dust,* and such recent films as *Home of the Brave, Lost Boundaries* and *Pinky,* in perspective. To direct an attack upon Hollywood would indeed be to confuse portrayal with action, image with reality. In the beginning was not the shadow, but the act, and the province of Hollywood is not action, but illusion. Actually, the anti-Negro images of the films were (and are) acceptable because of the existence throughout the United States of an audience obsessed with an inner psychological need to view Negroes as less than men. Thus, psychologically and ethically, these negative images constitute justifications for all those acts, legal, emotional, economic and political, which we label Jim Crow. The anti-Negro image is thus a ritual object of which Hollywood is not the creator, but the manipulator. Its role has been that of justifying the widely held myth of Negro unhumanness and inferiority by offering entertaining rituals through which that myth could be reaffirmed.

The great significance of the definition of Lucas Beauchamp's role in *Intruder in the Dust* is that it makes explicit the nature of Hollywood's changed attitude toward Negroes. Form being, in the words of Kenneth Burke, "the psychology of the audience," what is taking place in the American movie patron's mind? Why these new attempts to redefine the Negro's role? What has happened to the audience's mode of thinking?

For one thing there was the war; for another there is the fact that the United States' position as a leader in the world affairs is shaken by its treatment of Negroes. Thus the thinking of white Americans is undergoing a process of change, and reflecting that change, we find that each of the films mentioned above deals with some basic and unusually negative assumption about Negroes: Are Negroes cowardly soldiers? (*Home of the Brave*); are Negroes the real polluters of the South? (*Intruder in the Dust*); have mulatto Negroes the right to pass as white, at the risk of having black babies, or if they have white-skinned children, of having to kill off their "white" identities by revealing to them that they are, alas, Negroes? (*Lost Boundaries*); and, finally, should Negro girls marry white men or—wonderful non sequitur—should they help their race? (*Pinky*).

Obviously these films are not *about* Negroes at all; they are about what whites think and feel about Negroes. And if they are taken as accurate reflectors of that thinking, it becomes apparent that there is much confusion. To make use of Faulkner's metaphor again, the film makers fell upon the eggshell ice but, unlike the child, weren't heavy enough to break it. And, being unable to break it, they were unable to discover the real direction of their film narratives. In varying degree, they were unwilling to dig into the grave to expose the culprit, and thus we find them using ingenious devices for evading the full human rights of their Negroes. The result represents a defeat not only of drama, but of purpose.

In *Home of the Brave,* for instance, a psychiatrist tells the Negro soldier that his hysterical paralysis is like that of any other soldier who has lived when his friends have died; and we hear the soldier pronounced cured; indeed, we see him walk away prepared to open a bar and restaurant with a white veteran. But here there is an evasion (and by *evasion* I refer to the manipulation of the audience's attention away from reality to focus it upon false issues), because the guilt from which the Negro is supposed to suffer springs from an incident in which, immediately after his friend has called him a "yellowbelly nigger," he has wished the friend dead—only to see the wish granted by a sniper's bullet.

What happens to this racial element in the motivation of his guilt? The psychiatrist ignores it, and becomes a sleight-of-hand artist who makes it vanish by repeating again that the Negro is like everybody else. Nor, I believe, is this accidental, for it is here exactly that we come to the question of whether Negroes can rightfully be expected to risk their lives in an army in which they are slandered and discriminated against. Psychiatry is not, I'm afraid, the answer. The soldier suffers from concrete acts, not hallucinations.

From the motion picture *Home of the Brave.* Courtesy of United Artists.

And so with the others. In *Lost Boundaries* the question evaded is whether a mulatto Negro has the right to practice the old American pragmatic philosophy of capitalizing upon one's assets. For after all, whiteness *has* been given an economic and social value in our culture; and for the doctor upon whose life the film is based "passing" was the quickest and most certain means to success.

Yet Hollywood is uncertain about his right to do this. The film does not render the true circumstances. In real life Dr. Albert Johnson, the Negro doctor who "passed" as white, purchased the thriving practice of a deceased physician in Gorham, New Hampshire, for a thousand dollars. Instead, a fiction is introduced in the film wherein Dr. Carter's initial motivation for "passing" arises after he is refused an internship by dark Negroes in an Atlanta hospital—because of his color! It just isn't real, since there are thousands of mulattoes living as Negroes in the South, many of them Negro leaders. The only functional purpose served by this fiction is to gain sympathy for Carter by placing part of the blame for his predicament upon black Negroes. Nor should the irony be missed that part of the sentiment evoked when the Carters are welcomed back into the community is gained by painting Negro life as horrible, a fate worse than a living death. It would seem that in the eyes of Hollywood, it is only "white" Negroes who ever suffer—or is it merely the "white" corpuscles of their blood?

Pinky, for instance, is the story of another suffering mulatto, and the suffering grows out of a confusion between race and love. If we attempt to reduce the heroine's problem to sentence form we'd get something like this: "Should white-skinned Negro girls marry white men, or should they inherit the plantations of old white artistocrats (provided they can find any old aristocrats to will them their plantations) or should they live in the South and open nursery schools for black Negroes?" It doesn't follow, but neither does the action. After sitting through a film concerned with interracial marriage, we see it suddenly become a courtroom battle over whether Negroes have the right to inherit property.

Pinky wins the plantation, and her lover, who has read of the fight in the Negro press, arrives and still loves her, race be hanged. But now Pinky decides that to marry him would "violate the race" and that she had better remain a Negro. Ironically, nothing is said about the fact that her racial integrity, whatever that is, was violated before she was born. Her parents are never mentioned in the film. Following the will of the white aristocrat, who, before dying, advises her to "be true to herself," she opens a school for darker Negroes.

But in real life the choice is not between loving or denying one's race. Many couples manage to intermarry without violating their integrity, and indeed their marriage becomes the concrete expression of their integrity. In the film Jeanne Crain floats about like a sleepwalker, which seems to me to be exactly the way a girl so full of unreality would act. One thing is certain: no one is apt to mistake her for a Negro, not even a white one.

And yet, despite the absurdities with which these films are laden, they are all worth seeing, and if seen, capable of involving us emotionally. That they do is testimony to the deep centers of American emotion that they touch. Dealing with matters which, over the years, have been slowly charging up with guilt, they all display a vitality which escapes their slickest devices. And, naturally enough, one of the most interesting experiences connected with viewing them in predominantly white audiences is the profuse flow of tears and the sighs of profound emotional catharsis heard on all sides. It is as though there were some deep relief to be gained merely from seeing these subjects projected upon the screen.

It is here precisely that a danger lies. For the temptation toward self-congratulation which comes from seeing these films and sharing in their emotional release is apt to blind us to the true nature of what is unfolding—or failing to unfold—before our eyes. As an antidote to the sentimentality of these films, I suggest that they be seen in predominantly Negro audiences. For here, when the action goes phony, one will hear derisive laughter, not sobs. (Perhaps this is what Faulkner means about Negroes keeping the white man's conscience.) Seriously, *Intruder in the Dust* is the only film that could be shown in Harlem without arousing unintended laughter. For it is the only one of the four in which Negroes can make complete identification with their screen image. Interestingly, the factors that make this identification possible lie in its depiction not of racial but of human qualities.

Yet in the end, turning from art to life, we must even break with the definition of the Negro's role given us by Faulkner. For when it comes to conscience, we know that in this world each of us, black and white alike, must become the keeper of his own. This, in the deepest sense, is what these four films, taken as a group, should help us realize.

Faulkner himself seems to realize it. In the book *Intruder in the Dust,* Lucas attempts not so much to be the keeper of anyone else's conscience as to preserve his own life. Chick, in aiding Lucas, achieves that view of truth on which his own conscience depends.

"Intruder in the Dust"
Another Evasive Film on the Negro

Jose Yglesias

(*The Daily Worker,* November 23, 1949)

The movie version of William Faulkner's "Intruder In the Dust," which opened yesterday at the Mayfair, is a melodrama which appears to be about the Negro. In reality it is a whodunit and only involves the audience in the same old suspense—will the innocent man be cleared, will the murderer be found out? Were its portraits of Negroes not stereotype, its picture of the South false, its implications politically reactionary, it would alone betray its shallowness by the use of so spurious a formula to treat a serious theme.

In a small town in the Deep South an old Negro is arrested for the murder of a white man and immediately a lynch mob gathers. A white boy, who had once had an encounter with the Negro, decides to help him. An old white woman joins him, and the two, with a Negro boy whom they've forced to come along, dig up the white man's grave to check on the caliber of the bullet that killed him.

This first adventure leads to two or three turns of plot that finally clear the old Negro and uncover the real murderer. Like the lynch mob, which waits patiently for a day and a half in front of the jail, the question of Jimcrow and lynch law waits to be faced squarely, evaluated and judged in the movie. It never happens, except obliquely in the speeches of the town's lawyer. He makes of Negro oppression a moral question for middle class whites.

The virtues of "Intruder in the Dust" are few and incidental. It suggests gently what is brutal common knowledge—that legal justice works reluctantly for the Negro. It shows a lynch mob—though, as was said of the mob in "Pinky," it is one which "mumbles but doesn't molest." It has a central Negro character who, mainly through Juano Hernandez's projection, is a dignified and proud human being. And, filmed in Oxford, Mississippi, it is photographically realistic.

But these pinpoints of reality that break through the surface of the formula are more than flattened out by a host of other matters. The only other Negro character is a frightened Negro boy whose responses are all couched in the stereotype of the cowardly Negro. The actions of the mob and the anti-Negro chauvinisms of most of the characters are presented in a curiously neutral fashion: had the Negro in fact shot the white man, lynch law, it would follow, should be natural and justified.

The vague philosophizing and moral concerns of the lawyer, in a story that already presents Negroes as passive, are calculated to weaken any organized struggle against Jimcrow. Conceding a certain irony, not too explicit, in his statements, what is one to make of such conclusions as "We were in trouble, not Lucas."—meaning the Negro? Or this final axiom that everything will be all right in the South as long as "one of us doesn't run away." The movie advances the ludicrous idea that the agents of social progress will be old women and young boys since they are the only ones not thoroughly poisoned with white chauvinism.

Ben Maddow, the script's author, has excised the novel's blatant reactionary speeches and inner monologues (Hands off, you Yankees, Faulkner in effect said, we homogeneous race of Southerners will solve this problem), but Maddow has also slighted many of its insights into the involved anti-Negro psychology of Southerners. His economical and taut script begins brilliantly and runs a downhill course as the lynching theme is limited and distorted. After its challenging opening scene of a Southern town preparing itself for a lynching, "Intruder in the Dust" becomes an attempt, through the formula of the melodrama, to reassure us that everything is all right in the South.

Life Straight in de Eye

James Baldwin

(*Commentary* magazine, January 1955)

Hollywood's peculiar ability to milk, so to speak, the cow and the goat at the same time—and then to peddle the results as ginger ale—has seldom produced anything more arresting than the present production of *Carmen Jones.* In Hollywood, for example, immorality and evil (which are synonyms in that lexicon) are always vividly punished, though it is the way of the transgressor—hard perhaps but far from unattractive—which keeps us on the edge of our seats, and the transgressor himself—or herself—who engages all our sympathy. Similarly, in *Carmen Jones,* the implicit parallel between an amoral Gypsy and an amoral Negro woman is the entire root idea of the show; but at the same time, bearing in mind the distances covered since *The Birth of a Nation,* it is important that the movie always be able to repudiate any suggestion that Negroes are amoral—which it can only do, considering the role of the Negro in the national psyche, by repudiating any suggestion that Negroes are not white. With a story like *Carmen* interpreted by a Negro cast this may seem a difficult assignment, but Twentieth Century-Fox has brought it off. At the same time they have also triumphantly *not* brought it off, that is to say that the story *does* deal with amoral people, Carmen is a baggage, and it *is* a Negro cast.

This is made possible in the first place, of course, by the fact that *Carmen* is a "classic" or a "work of art" or something, therefore sacrosanct, and, luckily, quite old: it is as ludicrously unenlightened to accuse Mérimée or Bizet of having dirty minds as it is impossible to accuse them of being anti-Negro. (Though it *is* possible perhaps to accuse them of not knowing much and caring less about Gypsies.) In the second place the music helps, for it has assuredly never sounded so bald, or been sung so badly, or had less relevance to life, anybody's life, than in this production. The lyrics, too, in their way, help, being tasteless and vulgar in a way, if not to a degree, which cannot be called characteristic of Negroes. The movie's lifeless unreality is only occasionally threatened by Pearl Bailey, who has, however, been forestalled by Mr. Preminger's direction and is reduced—in a series of awful costumes, designed, it would appear, to camouflage her personality—to doing what is certainly the best that can be done with an abomination called *Beat Out That Rhythm on a Drum* and delivering her lines for the rest of the picture with such a murderously amused disdain that one cannot quite avoid the suspicion that she is commenting on the film. For a second or so at a time she escapes the film's deadly inertia and in Miss Bailey one catches glimpses of the imagination which might have exploded this movie into something worth seeing.

But this movie, more than any movie I can remember having seen, cannot afford, dare not risk, imagination. The "sexiness," for example, of Dorothy Dandridge, who plays Carmen, becomes quite clearly manufactured and even rather silly the moment Pearl Bailey stands anywhere near her.[1] And the moment one wishes that Pearl Bailey were playing Carmen one understands that *Carmen Jones* is controlled by another movie which Hollywood was studiously *not* making. For, while it is amusing to parallel Bizet's amoral Gypsy with a present-day, lower-class Negro woman, it is a good deal less amusing to parallel the Bizet violence with the violence of the Negro ghetto.

To avoid this—to exploit, that is, Carmen as a brown-skinned baggage but to avoid even suggesting any of the motivations such a present-day Carmen might have—it was helpful, first of all, that the script failed to require the services of any white people. This seals the action off, as it were, in a vacuum in which the spectacle of color is divested of its danger. The color itself then becomes a kind of vacuum which each spectator will fill with his own fantasies. But *Carmen Jones* does not inhabit the never-never land of such bogus but rather entertaining works as *Stormy Weather* or *Cabin in the Sky*—in which at least one could listen to the music; *Carmen Jones* has moved into a stratosphere rather more interesting and more pernicious, in which even Negro speech is parodied out of its charm and liberalized, if one may so put it, out of its force and precision. The result is not that the characters sound like everybody else, which would be bad enough; the result is that they sound ludicrously false and affected, like ante-bellum Negroes imitating their masters. This is also the way they look, and also rather the way they are dressed, and the word that springs immediately to mind to describe the appallingly technicolored sets—an army camp, a room, and a street on Chicago's South Side, presumably, which Bigger Thomas would certainly fail to recognize—is spotless. They could easily have been dreamed up by someone determined to prove that Negroes are as "clean" and as "modern" as white people and, I suppose, in one way or another, that is exactly how they *were* dreamed up.

And one is not allowed to forget for an instant that one is watching an opera, a word apparently synonymous in Mr. Preminger's mind with tragedy *and* fantasy, and the tone of *Carmen Jones* is stifling: a wedding of the blank, lofty solemnity with which Hollywood so often approaches "works of art" and the

---

1.　I have singled out Miss Bailey because the quality of her personality, forthright and wry, and with the authoritative ring of authenticity, highlights for me the lack of any of these qualities, or any positive qualities at all, in the movie itself. She is also the only performer with whose work I am more or less familiar. Since even she is so thoroughly handicapped by the peculiar necessities of *Carmen Jones,* I should like to make it clear that, in discussing the rest of the cast, I am not trying to judge their professional competence, which, on the basis of this movie—they do not even sing in their own voices—it would be quite unfair to do.

really quite helpless condescension with which Hollywood has always handled Negroes. The fact that one is watching a Negro cast interpreting *Carmen* is used to justify their remarkable vacuity, their complete improbability, their total divorce from anything suggestive of the realities of Negro life. On the other hand, the movie cannot possibly avoid depending very heavily on a certain quaintness, a certain lack of inhibition taken to be typical of Negroes, and further, the exigencies of the story—to say nothing of the images, which we will discuss in a moment—make it necessary to watch this movie, holding in the mind three disparate ideas: (1) that this is an opera having nothing to do with the present day, hence nothing, *really*, to do with Negroes; but (2) the greater passion, that winning warmth (of which the movie exhibits not a trace) so typical of Negroes makes *Carmen* an ideal vehicle for their graduation into Art; and (3) these are *exceptional* Negroes, as American, that is, as you and me, interpreting lower-class Negroes of whom they, also, are very fond, an affection which is proven perhaps by the fact that everyone appears to undergo a tiny, strangling death before resolutely substituting "de" for "the."

A movie is, literally, a series of images and what one *sees* in a movie can really be taken, beyond its stammering or misleading dialogue, as the key to what the movie is actually involved in saying. *Carmen Jones* is one of the first and most explicit—and far and away the most self-conscious—weddings of sex and color which Hollywood has yet turned out. (It will most certainly not be the last.) From this point of view the color wheel in *Carmen Jones* is very important. Dorothy Dandridge—Carmen—is a sort of taffy-colored girl, very obviously and vividly dressed, but really in herself rather more sweet than vivid. One feels— perhaps one is meant to feel—that here is a *very* nice girl making her way in movies by means of a bad-girl part; and the glow thus caused, especially since she is a colored girl, really must make up for the glow which is missing from the performance she is clearly working very hard at. Harry Belafonte is just a little darker and just as blankly handsome and fares very badly opposite her in a really offensive version of an already unendurable role. Olga James is Micaela, here called Cindy Lou, a much paler girl than Miss Dandridge but also much plainer, who is compelled to go through the entire movie in a kind of tearful stoop. Joe Adams is Husky Miller (Escamillo) and he is also rather taffy-colored, but since he is the second lead and by way of being the villain, he is not required to be as blank as Mr. Belafonte and there is therefore, simply in his presence, some fleeting hint of masculine or at least boyish force. For the rest, Pearl Bailey is quite dark and she plays, in effect, a floozie. The wicked sergeant who causes Joe to desert the army—in one of many wildly improbable scenes—and who has evil designs on Carmen is very dark indeed and so is Husky Miller's trainer, who is, one is given to suppose, Miss Bailey's sugar-daddy. It is quite clear that these people do not live in the same world with Carmen, or Joe, or Cindy Lou. All three of the leads are presented as indefinably complex and tragic, not after money or rhinestones but something else which causes them to be misunder- stood by the more earthy types around them. This something else is love, of course, and it is with the handling of this love story that the movie really goes to town.

It is true that no one in the original *Carmen,* least of all Carmen and her lover, are very clearly motivated, but there it scarcely matters because the opera is able to get by on a purely theatrical excitement, a sort of papier-maché violence, and the intense, if finally incredible, sexuality of its heroine. The movie does not have any of this to work with, since here excitement or violence could only blow the movie to bits, and, while the movie certainly indicates that Carmen is a luscious lollipop, it is on rather more uncertain ground when confronted with the notion of how attractive *she* finds men, and it cannot, in any case, use this as a motivating factor. Carmen is thus robbed at a stroke of even her fake vitality and all her cohesiveness and has become, instead, a nice girl, if a little fiery, whose great fault—and, since this is a tragedy, also her triumph—is that she looks at "life," as her final aria states it, "straight in de eye." In lieu of sexuality the movie-makers have dreamed up some mumbo jumbo involving buzzards wings, signs of the zodiac, and death-dealing cards, so that, it appears, Carmen ruins Joe because she loves him and decides to leave him because the cards tell her she is going to die. The fact that between the time she leaves him and the time he kills her she acquires some new clothes, and drinks—as one of her arias rather violently indicates she intends to—a great deal of champagne is simply a sign of her intense inner suffering.

From the motion picture *Carmen Jones.* Courtesy of Films Inc.—20th Century Fox.

Carmen has come a long way from the auction block, but Joe, of course, cannot be far behind. This Joe is a good, fine-looking boy who loves his Maw, has studied hard, and is going to be sent to flying school, and who is engaged to a girl who rather resembles his Maw, named Cindy Lou. His indifference to Carmen, who has all the other males in sight quivering with a passion never seen on land or sea, sets her ablaze; in a series of scenes which it is difficult to call erotic without adding that they are also infantile, she goes after him and he falls. Here the technicolored bodies of Dandridge and Belafonte, while the movie is being glum about the ruin of Joe's career and impending doom, are used for the maximum erotic effect. It is a sterile and distressing eroticism, however, because it is occurring in a vacuum between two mannequins who clearly are not involved in anything more serious than giving the customers a run for their money. One is not watching either tenderness or love and one is certainly not watching the complex and consuming passion which leads to life or death—one is watching a timorous and vulgar misrepresentation of these things.

And it must be said that one of the reasons for this is that, while the movie-makers are pleased to have Miss Dandridge flouncing about in tight skirts and plunging necklines—which is not exactly sexuality, either—the Negro male is still too loaded a quantity for them to know quite how to handle. The result is that Mr. Belafonte is really not allowed to do anything more than walk around looking like a spaniel: *his* sexuality is really taken as given because Miss Dandridge wants him. It does not, otherwise, exist and he is not destroyed by his own sexual aggressiveness, which he is not allowed to have, but by the sexual aggressiveness of the girl—or, as it turns out, not even really by that, but by tea leaves. The only reason, finally, that the eroticism of *Carmen Jones* is more potent than, say, the eroticism of a Lana Turner vehicle is because *Carmen Jones* has Negro bodies before the camera and Negroes are associated in the public mind with sex. Since darker races always seem to have for lighter races an aura of sexuality this fact is not distressing in itself. What is distressing is the conjecture this movie leaves one with as to what Americans take sex to be.

The most important thing about this movie—and the reason that, despite itself, it is one of the most important all-Negro movies Hollywood has yet produced—is that the questions it leaves in the mind relate less to Negroes than to the interior life of Americans. One wonders, it is true, if Negroes are really going to become the ciphers this movie makes them out to be, but, since they have until now survived public images even more appalling, one is encouraged to hope, for their sake and the sake of the Republic, that they will continue to prove themselves incorrigible. Besides, life does not produce ciphers like these: when people have become this empty they are not ciphers any longer, but monsters. The creation of such ciphers proves, however, that Americans are far from empty; they are, on the contrary, very deeply disturbed. And this disturbance is not the kind which can be eased by the doing of good works, but seems to have turned inward and shows every sign of becoming personal. This is one of the best things that can possibly happen. It can be taken to mean—among a great many other things—that the ferment which has resulted in as odd a brew as *Carmen Jones* can now be expected to produce something which will be more bitter on the tongue but sweeter in the stomach.

FOR DISCUSSION

1. What is your reaction to the article from *Opportunity*, 1929, concerning the increasing job market for Blacks in the Hollywood film industry? Its author, Floyd Covington, an Urban League executive, sees movies as a useful source of employment for Blacks, and never once complains about the roles assigned them. Indeed, he looks forward to the coming of all-Negro features, which other writers on this subject have bitterly complained about. In what way does Covington's job orientation reflect national attitudes about material progress in the late 1920s? Should some positive recognition be given to Hollywood for its consistent employment of Black actors over the years, regardless of the roles in which they were cast? Why or why not?

2. In his evaluation of the all-Black film, *Hearts in Dixie*, Robert Benchley has unalloyed praise for the "amazing personality of Stepin Fetchit," whose "voice ... manner ... timing" are "near to perfection." Compare Benchley's praise to the criticism of Fetchit by Black critics in this section. (Also consider Ossie Davis's explanation of the Stepin Fetchit image on pp. 1–2.)

3. Benchley also praises "the White dialogue writers who ... have given the Negroes a better break than they have given themselves in the past." Benchley was a top-flight humorist and could certainly tell when lines were well-handled or not, but how might his own feeling about the dialogue of *Hearts in Dixie* be right only for White audiences? And why might Black dialogue writers do a bad job in the kinds of pieces Benchley refers to? (Who was the audience for them?)

4. Generally speaking, after reading through the criticism of the Stepin Fetchit and Hattie McDaniels "stock" roles of the '30s and '40s, what do you think their most negative aspect was? How do such portrayals (lazy, stupid, blindly loyal, musical, etc.) affect Whites and Blacks viewing these films?

5. In his essay, "The Shadow and the Act," Ralph Ellison discusses four films concerning Blacks released in the late 1940s. Although all of the films have serious, generally pro-Negro intentions, only one, *Intruder in the Dust*, could, according to Ellison, meet the approval of a totally Black audience. After seeing *Intruder in the Dust* (which needs to be screened in a unit of this kind) or reading Faulkner's novel, analyze the character of Lucas Beauchamp. How far removed is he from the Stepin Fetchit image, and why does Ellison see this role as something of a landmark in

Hollywood's portrayal of a Black man? Can a case be made against the characterization of Beauchamp for merely serving as a vehicle to bring out the best qualities of the Whites? Consider the difference if Faulkner's Black had actually killed the White man (certainly he would have had cause) and the film then had to deal with the consciences of the Whites trying to understand the Black man's guilt. Compare the review of *Intruder in the Dust* by Jose Yglesias from the Communist paper, *The Daily Worker*, with Ellison's. Which statement about the film best does it justice?

6.   After reading the articles in this section, consider all the factors they have in common. What are the overriding complaints of the authors against the Hollywood dream factory? What kinds of solutions to the problem are they generally agreed upon, if any? Which of the critiques was most effective in sensitizing you to the impact of stereotyped portrayals of Blacks in movies? Why?

PART FOUR

A "New" Image for the Future?

Within about the last decade, the screen image of the Black man has changed considerably since the days of Stepin Fetchit. This new image has been largely due to the public acceptance of Sidney Poitier as the first full-fledged Black movie "star." The heroic image of Poitier in such films as *The Defiant Ones, A Raisin in the Sun, Lilies of the Field, In the Heat of the Night,* and others, has been highly praised by film critics and social reformers. Former *New York Times* critic, Bosley Crowther's laudatory appraisal of Poitier is a fairly typical one.

Recently, however, the Poitier image has received objections from a small but vocal minority. The complaints of these anti-Poitier forces insist that the actor is bogged down in a new kind of stereotype, as articulated in the article by Clifford Mason.

The remainder of this section includes the views of two critics, one Black (Lindsay Patterson) and one White (Renata Adler), on the first American film attempting to depict Black militancy, *Up Tight* (a remake of *The Informer,* a classic film about the Irish rebellion).

The Significance of Sidney

Bosley Crowther

(*The New York Times,* August 6, 1967)

The emergence of Sidney Poitier through a long and distinguished career as the most conspicuous and respected exponent of the American Negro on the screen is a categorical distinction I rather imagine he may privately eschew and one which might well be resented by more militant members of his race. For, of course, it is not the most exalting tribute to an artist to say that he is the best there is at representing or expressing within a limited range. It might sound like the left-handed compliment the young son of friends of mine paid himself when he wrote home from camp to inform them he was the best swimmer in the non-swimmer group.

And, further, there is a strong feeling among some battlers against racial lines that there should be no racial distinctions among the characters in a play or a film, that it shouldn't make any difference whether an actor is white or black. These people would say no one is likely to proclaim that any particular actor is the most conspicuous and respected exponent of the American white man on the screen. Therefore why should Mr. Poitier be commended on the basis of race?

There is no question that these militants have a good theoretical point, and the day should come when recognition of coloration will be nil. But with things as they are at present, with race consciousness being as strong as it is and with tragedies happening daily because of activation of issues of race, it is thoroughly unreasonable to imagine that audiences could be color blind, or that dramas exposing the reality of racial distinctions should be dismissed.

Indeed, the misfortune at this moment—as it has been all along—is that first-class films of racial problems are so few and far between. One of the symptoms, if not a cause, of the white man's long complacency about and distaste for the troubles of the Negro population has been his general indifference to films that have tried to show something of these troubles and urge some compassion towards them.

One can ruefully remember a pitiful handful of excellent films that have put forth some very powerful warnings on racial injustice and prejudice that did not receive the attendance or even the social attention they deserved. The most deplorably neglected was the film version of William Faulkner's novel, "Intruder in the Dust," which had the splendid actor, Juano Hernandez (who remembers him?), in the focal role of a Negro leader threatened with lynching in a Mississippi town.

The very fact that the films about Negroes have been so low on the popularity scale is all the more reason for delighting in the emergence of Mr. Poitier to the eminence he has as an artist and as an exponent of his race. But it should be noted clearly that he first came to attention and established his name in films where he played an individual Negro fighting for position among whites.

It was in such excellent performances as that which he gave in "The Defiant Ones" as a Negro convict escaping from a chaingang shackled to a white, or as the one Negro high school student among a clutter of white hooligans in "The Blackboard Jungle," or as the racially oppressed doctor in "No Way Out," that he made an impression upon the public that paradoxically passed him up when he gave an equally good performance in the virtually all-Negro film, "A Raisin in the Sun."

And, of course, it should be noted that he won his Academy award for playing a spiritually-chastened servant to a group of impoverished nuns in that charming but sentimental parable of brotherly love, "Lilies of the Field."

Thus it is most appropriate and gratifying to see Mr. Poitier coming out at this moment of crisis in racial affairs in a film which impressively presents him as a splendid exponent of his race, maturely able to stand up to the abuse and patronage of racist whites. This is his brilliant appearance as a northern police detective who happens to be picked up in a Mississippi town on the night of the murder of an important white man in the drama, "In the Heat of the Night."

What is inspiring about it is that he rises with passionate dignity to the ugly, contemptuous challenge of his competence thrown down by the local chief of police who finds he must have the assistance (or the scapegoat excuse) of anyone—even an "uppity nigger"—in trying to solve the case. With a firm and ferocious authority of a quality that he has seldom shown—he certainly is not called upon to show it in his also current homily, "To Sir, With Love"—Mr. Poitier faced down the bogey of all the southern red-neck cops we've ever known, this one performed by Rod Steiger in a composite that fairly oozes swear and hate. And in the end he comes out with a significant token of respect—not acceptance, but respect—from the policeman. In this day and film, that's a lot.

Why Does White America
Love Sidney Poitier So?

Clifford Mason
(*The New York Times*, September 10, 1967)

There are two Sidney Poitiers. One is the man dedicated to the improvement of the Negro image in general and to rectifying the wrongs perpetrated against black women in particular. The other is the Negro movie star that all white America loves. And why do they love him so? Because he's a good actor? Partly. Because he's worked hard to get where he is? Maybe. Because he stands for a proud, black image, something all of us who are non-white have needed in this country for a long, long, time? Noooooo.

But then the question of what makes for a proud image and what makes for a demeaning one is itself open to all sorts of argument. It seems this is the year for cliches in theatrical thought. According to a recent interview, Mr. Poitier had trouble with his conscience or self-respect or whatever, in making both "Porgy and Bess" and "The Long Ships." And yet there is no record of his feeling similar misgivings in doing things like "Lilies of the Field," "A Patch of Blue," "The Bedford Incident," "Duel at Diablo," or "To Sir With Love."

I submit that the Negro (or black, if you will) image was subverted by his roles in these films much more so than it was in the two films he seems worried about. Honesty is still the most important ingredient in art. The black writer Loften Mitchell has said that Arthur Miller's "Death of a Salesman" would have been an even greater play had Miller in fact used his Jewishness as forthrightly as O'Neill used his Irishness in "Long Day's Journey into Night." And it is a schizophrenic flight from identity and historical fact that makes anybody imagine, even for a moment, that the Negro is best served by being a black version of the man in the gray flannel suit, taking on white problems and a white man's sense of what's wrong with the world.

I, too, am tired of "Porgy and Bess." But at least it doesn't try to fool us. Even though its Negroes are frankly stereotypes, at least we have a man, a real man, fighting for his woman and willing to follow her into the great unknown, the big city, poor boy from Catfish Row that he is. What did we have in "The Bedford Incident," by comparison? Poitier as a black correspondent who went around calling everyone sir. Did anyone ever see Gary Cooper or Greg Peck call anyone sir when *they* played foreign correspondents? And after Richard Widmark (who starred with Poitier in the film) barks at him and pushes him around all over the submarine for almost two hours, the only thing he gets to do at the end is shout at bad Dicky Widmark. And why do they allow him to shout at Widmark? Because Widmark has just gotten the whole ship stuck in the path

From the motion picture *The Defiant Ones.* Courtesy of United Artists.

of an onrushing torpedo that blows them all to heaven the next instant! For that kind of mistake, Poitier should at least have been allowed to bust him one in the jaw.

And yet, listening to the things Poitier says, one wonders if he would have thought it appropriate. In "Duel at Diablo" he did little more than hold James Garner's hat, and this after he had won the Academy Award. What white romantic actor would take a part like that? He gets to kill a few Indians, but Garner gets the girl and does all the real fighting. Poitier was simply dressed up in a fancy suit, with a cigar stuck in his mouth and a new felt hat on his head.

"To Sir, With Love" had the all-time Hollywood reversal act. Instead of putting a love interest into a story that had none, they took it out. But "A Patch of Blue" was probably the most ridiculous film Poitier ever made. He's a newspaper reporter who befriends a blind white girl from the slums, a girl whom he doesn't even make love to. He gets her away from her whoring mother and sends her off to a home for the blind, and the little symbolism at the end with the music box makes it clear that they'll never see each other again. And why does he go to the park day after day and sit with her and string beads and buy her lunch? Because he's running his private branch of the ASPCA, the Black Society for the Prevention of Cruelty to Blind White Girls, the BSPCBWG?

All this Mr. Poitier endures, and more, without a murmur of protest. Now there are those who will say there's nothing else he can do. *They* won't let him make anything else. I used to console myself with the fact that that was probably true. And it may very well be true. But truer than that is the fact that he thinks these films have really been helping to change the stereotypes that black actors are subjected to. In essence, they are merely contrivances, completely lacking in any real artistic merit. In all of these films he has been a showcase nigger, who is given a clean suit and a complete purity of motivation so that, like a mistreated puppy, he has all the sympathy on his side and all those mean whites are just so many Simon Legrees.

Gradualism may have some value in politics. But in art it just represents a stale, hackneyed period, to be forgotten as soon as we can get on to the real work at hand. And artistic NAACPism is all that this whole period of Sidney Poitier moviemaking stands for. At least the villain he played in "The Long Ships" was a fighter—on his own mission, in his own world. And even though there was the nonsense about a vow that kept him from making love to Rossana Schiaffino, her attempt to warn him of danger and his death at Richard Widmark's hands were handled with great care for the importance of his role. He was not killed as a mean, despicable villain, but rather as a noble enemy. Even more important, he was nobody's eunuch or black mammy busting his gut for white folks as if their problems were all that's important in the world. And so the stern "I hated it" that he uttered in a recent interview to tell how he felt about doing "The Long Ships" shows the confusion in his mind as to what constitutes dignity for Negroes in films.

The rabid rumor—indeed, it's an incontestable fact by now—that Poitier actually kisses the white girl *and* marries her in his next opus, "Guess Who's Coming to Dinner," should presumably refute all of my arguments up to this

From the motion picture **Guess Who's Coming to Dinner?** Courtesy of Columbia Pictures.

point. But what should seem obvious is that the prime concern is not with the manipulation of black and white bodies before the camera. So close today and closer tomorrow. They can give him the girl, all the girls, and have him kill ten rednecks and still make a bad picture. And that is the essence of the argument. Until the concern of movies is for the dignity, the manhood, the thinking of the Negro in his world, with its historical past, its turbulent present and its hopeful future, there can be no true portrait of the Negro and no true art. Whites may or may not play a part in this world; the crucial need however is for a break with the concept that the world is only white, and that the Negro exists only in the white man's view of him.

Now Poitier may very well say that he is sacrificing his career so that eventually all God's chillun will be able to do what white folks been doing for years. That would be a cute point, and I'd like to think it *was* true. But until the day of complete honesty comes, white critics will gladly drag out a double standard and applaud every "advance" in movies like "Lilies of the Field" as so much American-style, democratic goodwill. Which is what the road to hell is paved with.

Finally—and this brings us completely up to date as far as Negroes in films are concerned, because Poitier is really all we have, there being room for only one of us at a time—there is "In the Heat of the Night." Even though the acting, his and Rod Steiger's particularly, is excellent, we have the same old Sidney Poitier syndrome: a good guy in a totally white world, with no wife, no sweetheart, no woman to love or kiss, helping the white man solve the white man's problem. True, the nature of his purpose is an improvement over what it was in "Lilies of the Field": there is some racial justification for his working to solve the murder in "In the Heat of the Night." The white victim was a Northerner who had planned to employ Negroes as well as whites in a factory in Mississippi. And this time out, Poitier actually gets to slap a white Southern aristocrat. Of course, he only does it after the aristocrat slaps *him.*

But he remains unreal, as he has for nearly two decades, playing essentially the same role, the antiseptic, one-dimensional hero. If he keeps it up, he'll soon be able to give Sean Connery lessons in how to do the same role year after year after year. I can just see the two of them now: Connery, toothless and doddering, but still killing Asians, Turks and some white Communists, while 50 girls try to get his courage up. And Poitier, finally going to flesh, but still pure, still nonplussed by white arrogance and wanting only to be left alone but, because of his innate goodness, finally making that fateful decision to solve the problem for "them," good nigger that he is.

It's Gonna Blow Whitey's Mind

Lindsay Patterson

(*The New York Times,* August 25, 1968)

Thank God there's no frock-coat Lawd thundering earthly platitudes ("How de fish fry goin'?"), or Catfish Row nonsense, or hallelujah singing for the benefit of the KKK, happening in Cleveland and Hollywood these days. It's kind of surprising. Some black folks—for a change—are getting a chance to tell it *somewhat* like it is, in, of all things, a multi-million dollar Technicolor Hollywood movie. What began as an updated all-black Harlem version of "The Informer," John Ford's 1935 classic about the secret Irish Republican Brotherhood, is now "Up Tight!", a sometimes ferocious story of today's black militants and nonviolence advocates, set in the Hough area of Cleveland—as shabby and dilapidated a black ghetto as likely to be found anywhere.

But before anyone gets the wonderful idea that Hollywood has a guilty conscience and has finally conceded a racial crisis does exist in our country, it should be explained that Paramount Pictures originally wanted director Jules Dassin to remake "The Informer" with an all-white cast. Failing that, the studio settled for Dassin and an all-black cast. Of course, it never occurred to anyone that a backlog of black material by black American writers exists, or that two of the greatest American novels, "Invisible Man" and "Native Son," have never been made into major motion pictures. So, instead of starting from scratch with young black writers or using existing black materials, "Up Tight!"—as so much else in our society concerning the black man—neatly compromises, by employing two of its stars, Ruby Dee and Julian Mayfield, along with Dassin, as co-authors.

Nevertheless, "Up Tight!", by Hollywood's feeble standards, is probably the most "daring" film ever to be in production, certainly in its admission that there is more to the racial crisis than one manicured black man pining to become acceptable to the white establishment, and that there are some blacks in the ghetto who are tired of whitey's "junk" ("He ain't never gonna change"), and are doing something about it in the only terms that whitey seemingly understands.

Structurally, the film follows rather straightforwardly the situation and plot lines of Liam O'Flaherty's "The Informer" and the movie John Ford made from it. Tank Williams (Julian Mayfield), a bumbling, weak-minded, strong-as-an-ox alcoholic, is expelled by a black militant organization for refusing to assist three members in stealing guns the night Martin Luther King is murdered (Tank is devastated by King's death and has taken to the bottle). One member of the trio kills a guard, and Tank is more or less persuaded by a brilliant, cynical, homosexual and paid police informer (Roscoe Lee Browne) to finger the gunman. Also, Tank feels deeply inadequate in not being able to support his girl friend (Ruby Dee), who, to make ends meet, resorts to part-time prostitution and welfare. After he informs, Tank's free spending of the reward-money causes suspicion and the members of the militant organization elicit from him a confession of guilt. The ending—a departure from the original, in which the informer is shot down by his former comrades—has Tank atoning for his guilt by jumping to his death from a bridge. Apparently, Dassin did not want to conclude "Up Tight!" with blacks killing other blacks.

Perhaps the most important moments in the film are the confrontations between the leader of the militant group, Raymond St. Jacques, and the leader of the moderate group, Frank Silvera, when each presents his case, the militant for guns and the moderate for education. The film avoids drawing a conclusion as to which program is more feasible (a mistake, I feel), but endeavors to dramatize what it sees as the two approaches open to blacks in white America.

Although the film does not wish to illustrate by concrete examples what either group can or cannot accomplish, the production unit, during its recent five weeks in Cleveland, found out what a local militant group can achieve through unilateral action. When filming began in the streets of the ghetto, the group demanded that a black policeman—whom they charged with brutality and the indiscriminate use of firepower in previous encounters—be removed from escort duty on the movie. Their demand ignored by city authorities, they initiated a campaign of "harassment" by systematically marching in circles around the policeman. The situation became tense, and the predominantly white, middle-class production crew panicked, walked off their jobs, threatening to return to Hollywood. After a highly charged meeting between the blacks and the whites of the production, it was agreed that the whites had "reacted excessively" to an internal ghetto affair. Raymond St. Jacques and other actors went on television and radio to ask the ghetto community to "keep cool." St. Jacques explained what the film was about, and pointed out that it had the "blessing" of Carl Stokes, the black mayor of Cleveland. To many militants, however, the production was another example of the "establishment" locking them out, denying them a "piece of the action." It was not until someone got the "bright" idea of employing a few members of the militant group that production resumed in another location in the Hough area without incident and without the previous contingent of police escorts.

When I visited one shooting location recently—an abandoned Pennsylvania Railroad station of a bygone era at 55th and Euclid—everything seemed, on the surface at least, to be going smoothly. There was a lively audience of ghetto residents (no police in sight) attentively watching a "black militant" fervently addressing a small crowd huddled in the rain at the edge of the station's promenade: "We got to get our own thing going, our own program . . ." The same scene had been tried unsuccessfully in heavy rain the previous night. This was a clear and cloudless night, and water sprinklers had been placed on the northeast corner of the station's roof and in other strategic spots to provide just enough rain. After nearly three hours, the scene was finally wrapped up. The actors (mostly real militants from the area), were drenched, yet ebullient. Julian Mayfield was part of the crowd.

A big, broad, confident man, Mayfield is known primarily as a novelist ("The Hit," "The Grand Parade"), but he did some stage acting "years ago," once as an understudy to a then fledgling young actor named Sidney Poitier in the Broadway musical "Lost in the Stars." Mayfield has been in a kind of "exile" from the United States because of his intensely militant political activity. He has spent the years since 1961 in Ghana (he was a speech writer for Nkrumah) and Spain, and only returned to this country in June of last year.

"I didn't lose touch by being away so long," insists Mayfield, when asked if his absence had handicapped him in working on a script about today's young militants. "Instead, I gained more of a perspective. People like Muhammed Ali and Malcolm X were constantly passing through Ghana, and I got from them firsthand what was going on back here. If I had been here, I would've only gotten my information from the newspapers."

While the younger actors in "Up Tight!" have great expectations for the movie (both in terms of their own careers and the impact it will make: "It's gonna blow whitey's mind"), the older generation is adopting a "wait and see" attitude. For the veteran black actor it is a too familiar scene, where hopes are raised only to be dashed cruelly by an indifferent white America. Ruby Dee offers perhaps the most sober view when she describes the film "as a good drop of water into that ocean."

Miss Dee—along with her husband Ossie Davis—has, for about two decades, led the fight for integration in the theater, and she is probably the only black actress to have worked with any degree of consistency in nonstereotyped dramatic roles ("A Raisin in the Sun," "Purlie Victorious"). Being a black performer in America, she feels, limits not only opportunities, but the ability to perform at full capacity.

"My own career," she says, "has not been as flourishing as I'd like because of things inside me which make me wary of experimenting with roles. Many black people have hurdles within themselves which they have to overcome before they can function at top efficiency. Thank God my own children are seemingly free of any restrictions."

Unlike many middle-class blacks and whites Miss Dee does not put down the rebellious younger generation, but lays its unrest squarely at the door of the "old folks." "Our young people have sensed that there is something lacking in *us.* They are rebelling against things they don't want. Too bad we live in a time when people have to destroy in order for us to listen. We seemingly can only listen under pain. The only time we move is after a tragedy."

Raymond St. Jacques, who has a mild reputation for flamboyant living (he likes to drive fast cars fast and serve brunches in flowing African robes in his $100,000 California house), will in all probability be the next black matinee idol. He has worked impressively as villains in "The Pawnbroker" and "The Comedians," and is being described as a "black Lee Marvin" ("I want to be a black Raymond St. Jacques!"). Currently in "The Green Berets," he will get star billing for the first time in "Up Tight!" Off screen, he is an advocate of both black power and the status quo.

"I am not interested in wrecking the establishment," he says. "I am only interested in building. I want to contribute to the social revolution in my own limited way. I tried to get black money when I started my picture corporation, but you know how impossible that was."

Nevertheless, the 6-foot-3-inch, former Yale drama student is clearly pleased about his healthy film career. Max Julien, a young Broadway actor (he plays the militant who shoots the guard while stealing guns), is also working like hell in Hollywood and determined to make it. But he is optimistic about the future of the black actor in Hollywood. "The door is open now," he says, "but will close after the elections in November. What we got to do now is swell the ranks so they can't close it all the way."

Some attitudes among black members of "Up Tight!" indicate something of the wide gulf separating blacks and whites. Many of the blacks suspect the technical crew (which includes three blacks) of "subconsciously" trying to sabotage the production, since "white hatred for the black man is so deep he can't help it." This has led to the conclusion by some that the film will never be released, because "it tries to deal too honestly with the black man, and whitey ain't never going to accept that."

Producer-director Dassin ("Never on Sunday," "Rififi," "He Who Must Die") says that upon his return to Hollywood for interior filming he will try to persuade other producers and directors to push for more enrollment of blacks into the craft unions. But Dassin, who has not made a movie in Hollywood since the McCarthy era, does not consider this production as marking his return to the film capital. "I will not make another movie in America," he declares.

Dassin has discovered (or re-discovered) that America is a maze of small bureaucratic minds that like nothing better than to exclude on the false issues of race, creed or religion. "Up Tight!", clearly, is a hopeful step toward a broader vision. If there is any courage at all in Hollywood it will be followed quickly by other steps, even bolder, so that more movies will tell it like it really is, without fear, for the good of us all.

Critic Keeps Her Cool on "Up Tight"

Renata Adler

(The New York Times, December 29, 1968)

It is possible that television reporting and newspapers have almost completely exhausted the old dramatic possibilities of the arts. It is not just a matter of photography infringing on representational painting, so that people no longer require an artist to record their faces for posterity. It is that a lot of the traditional options of drama—a distillation of life into crises, speculations about the lives of the great, the simple transmission and preservation of *news*—have gone over into instantaneous documentary. The only point in a play or a movie about the funeral of James Chaney, in 1964, would have been to recreate in imagination that scene for people who were not there to see and hear it.

But we were *all* there, with television and the press, that moment when David Dennis, a young black field secretary of CORE, said in a soft, breaking voice that he was sick and tired of funerals—when he enumerated Emmet Till, lynched, Mack Charles Parker, lynched, Medgar Evers, shot from behind, added "If you do go home tonight and take it, God damn your soul,"—and withdrew from the pulpit in tears, is there on film and in memory. It was one of the great, tragic scenes of our time. Before the media, people would have few, if any, such moments in their lives, and had to turn to literature and drama for the rest. Now we have them all, too many, in straight, fast transmission of events as they take place.

In trying to draw the emotional responses back, the most banal artists simply exaggerate, raising the threshold to extremes of misery or violence beyond what even reality has to offer. This doesn't work. You have to stylize. It is unlikely that a plain, "realistic" war or sentimental public film will ever succeed again. The ones that still work are films about private lives, essentially autobiography, that do not reach the media, good reporting, or imaginative, undocumentary breakthroughs of various kinds.

"Up Tight," a transposition by Jules Dassin of the plot of Liam O'Flaherty's "The Informer" to the black section of Cleveland, doesn't work, though the cast is black: Julian Mayfield, as an unemployed, drunken steelworker who is expelled from the committee of militants; Raymond St. Jacques, as an intellectual militant leader; Max Julien, as a fallen hero; Janet MacLachlan as his African haircut sister; Frank Silvera, as a believer in the system; Roscoe Lee Browne, as a homosexual collaborator with the police; Ruby Dee as a desperate young woman on welfare; Juanita Moore, as the hero's dying mother. And the idiom seems solid and good.

Yet the film is never for one instant moving, never lives up even to its initial documentary footage of the voice and funeral of Martin Luther King. (This failure is complicated by the fact that the footage is hoked up with shots of cheese in front of a television set, which makes no point really and simply ornaments and artifies the event.)

At its worst, when the characters are theatrically posed, it is as though everyone were about to burst into song and the film seems a drained, modernized "Porgy and Bess."

The film's problems are complicated by the fact that it is not true, that the reality of the Negro movement in this country lies elsewhere. There is no black revolution so far in the Irish "troubles" sense. Negro militant meetings and Black caucuses are much more complex than traditional party cells. It has not happened, and it does not make emotional sense to cast a black hero as a member of a violent revolution in progress and to star a discarded man who betrays him. It is not historically or foreseeably real. In fact, the whole black movement is too deep and complex to be treated—even in a first, and at heart admirable, effort to present some real Negro situation in a conventional film—in this particular way.

There is the nonviolence that swept out of the South, one of the great intellectual and moral forces of our time—which may still transform the country radically. It was and is dramatic and black. There is the movement in the North to educate the young, separately if need be, and create a historically unique intellectual community. There is the less dramatic effort to integrate with the white middle class. There are personal dramas unrelated to politics. There are all the manifestations of suffering, courage, achievement and despair. There are the Panthers, effective half at the level of fantasy, the black few's dream and the white few's nightmare. There just doesn't happen to be "The Informer." All the tricky confrontations in front of distorting mirrors at carnivals, all the compressed nearly balanced discussions of ideology won't make it fit. It fails in more than just being emotionally unequal to the documentary. It gets less audience response than "For Love of Ivy." And yet one can't help hoping that it has started something in films, and that truer versions will follow.

FOR DISCUSSION

1.   Critics Bosley Crowther and Clifford Mason take entirely different points of view on the significance of the career of Sidney Poitier as the first Black movie "star." After screening at least one of the Poitier films on which this debate is based, explain how you feel about the image the role(s) project. Should he be praised for his total rejection of the old stereotypes, or criticized for accepting roles which portray him as the "super Negro"? Is there any logical middle ground in this argument?

2.   Does an actor who has achieved the stature of Sidney Poitier now have a responsibility to work to achieve a broader integration of the film industry, particularly behind the scenes in actual movie production (scenarists, directors, cinematographers, etc.)? Would such action on his part be influential in creating other Black film stars as well as presenting a more realistic, human portrayal of Black people on the screen? Based on all that you've read in this anthology so far, do you feel Hollywood would be willing to go beyond the tokenism of one Black film star? Give your reasons.

3.   All of the articles in the section, regardless of their criticisms, agree that the film industry has changed its basic image of the Black man. He is no longer cast as a Stepin Fetchit. Today with actors like Poitier, Jim Brown and Raymond St. Jacques (the militant leader in *Up Tight*), the Black man has been more prominently portrayed as strong, dignified, and heroic. Considering the history of the portrayal of Blacks on the screen, what do you think are the fundamental reasons for the change in characterization? Is the new, heroic image a genuine sign that the motion picture industry has taken an enlightened, realistic view of American race relations, or is it something else?

4.   The following poem, written by a Black student, comments on the "new" Hollywood image:

> "Ta Dum Da Dum
> Dum Dum   Dum-Dum
> Ultra Black Uncle Tom
> Was a Star

(m   Gee!   m)
Cause
    he had
Answered the
Ha/ Lee/ wood
    Add
Wanted
Super Clean Dynamite
    Black Militant
    to play star/ ring
    role in movie
P. S.
    Must Be Willing
    to die at the end.
        by William Johnson

Do you share the author's opinion of this "new" image? Why or why not?

5.   Analyze the debate between Black critic Lindsay Patterson and White critic Renata Adler over their interpretations of the film, *Up Tight*, which deals with Black militancy. Cite some of the basic reasons for the differences between their opinions. If you have seen the film, comment on which critique is closest to your feelings about it and why.

PART FIVE

Beyond Sidney Poitier—
*Possible Solutions
and Trends for the Future*

Throughout this book we have examined the Black image in motion pictures and witnessed countless protests against the dishonesty of that image. The question still remains, however—what can be done about it? How can Blacks, and concerned Whites, persuade the film and television industries to start humanizing their products? This section presents a few suggestions as possible solutions.

Black composer, William Grant Still, writing in 1945 in *Opportunity*, skillfully analyzes the problems confronting Blacks in Hollywood during the World War II era. After surveying the problems, his conclusion is that Black economic pressure through boycotts of demeaning films could awaken the film industry to a realization of its slanderous actions. Despite the date of Still's suggestion, it is an attempt at a concrete solution, and as such, is worthy of consideration for today.

Militant author and social critic, Harold Cruse, writing more recently, also advocates a kind of boycott. His proposal, however, goes far beyond a mere economic boycott. Cruse advocates a Black cultural ethos and therefore a rejection of *all* White-conceived roles for Blacks in the mass media. Perhaps the rise of Black film producers is a step in this direction.

The final part of this section—a condensed article from *Newsweek* by Charles Michener—details the opinions of a number of Black performers and directors on the current Black movie explosion.

How Do We Stand in Hollywood?

William Grant Still

(*Opportunity Magazine,* 1945)

Quick to recognize the fact that films have a tremendous educational value both at home and abroad, allied governments have made excellent use of this medium to such an extent that Hollywood itself has boasted of this contribution to the war effort. If we concede that films do educate people in this way, we must also admit that they create lasting impressions in other matters—racial matters, for instance. In this respect, the Negro has been, with a very few exceptions, on the losing end of the deal and, despite the rare gestures of goodwill that have been made, the same old racial stereotypes continue to be perpetuated, the same old clichés abound.

The films' sins have been, in the main, those of omission rather than of commission, as far as the Negro is concerned. They have shown, with rare exceptions, only one side of Negro life to such an extent that one Negro writer, in desperation, begged for a Negro villain, just to break the stereotype! The Negro is willing to be portrayed on the screen in any truthful way, as long as aspiring Negro people are filmed along with the servants and the theatrical figures. The Negro doesn't want to be stuffy. He wants to laugh too, but until a few decent portrayals come along, he has to be a crusader. . . .

For the present, we would like to see ridiculous, criminal, superstitious and immoral characterizations eliminated; Negroes cast in other than servant roles; Negroes' contribution to the war and to American life pictured; Negroes included as extras in background groups; Negroes employed in studios in other positions than those of actor and menial; Negroes employed as authorities on the Negro. We would like to see all-Negro films abolished for, no matter how expensive and glamorous they are, they still glorify segregation. In short, we would like to see the Negro presented to the world and to America as a normal American. If this were done, the films could make a real contribution to inter-racial understanding and to a better world.

When one mentions these things to film people, they invariably say that they are in the entertainment business solely, and that they do not want to put out anything that may be considered a sociological study. That, of course, is logical, but it still does not explain why they are so proud of their educational work in other fields, and why they will not concede that such things can be done simply and without fanfare and the resulting films still be good entertainment.

Just now,[1] there is a good opportunity for advances as regards minority groups in films. The reason is, that among thinking people, there exists a more or

---

1. During World War II.

Reprinted with permission of the National Urban League, Inc.

less general understanding that one of the biggest issues to be settled in the present conflict is that of the status of minorities all over the world. This has caused a healthy wave of interest in a good many matters that were once thought to be taboo. Some few publishers are getting enough courage to bring out books and articles that would not have been tolerated a few years ago, and are finding them profitable.

The films, which on the one hand, are committed to a policy of non-controversial matters and, on the other hand, are united in a desire to present timely dramas, now find themselves in a peculiar position. The Negro on the American stage has always been a commercial success when he has been *good*. Therefore, he might be equally successful on the screen, provided, in Hollywood's opinion—and here comes the rub—those vociferous Negroes who write articles and take part in dramas would just be sensible and let Hollywood tell them how it ought to be done, for it is clear that Hollywood is not yet prepared to give up many of its cherished ideas. There are a great many reasons for this, reasons which may be understood better if we know just how the films function from the inside, with all the glamour of publicity agents' tales left out.

First of all, in the life of a motion picture, there are three stages. The first two, the making and distributing, are almost completely unknown to the general public. The third stage—the selling angle (which involves the work of the paid publicity agent) is the only one with which the public is familiar. Here's the procedure from the outset. When someone gets an idea for a picture, he must first sell it to a producer. If he goes to an independent company, this group has first of all to get a major release, for almost everyone has to go through one of the big companies nowadays. Then the producer has to get what is called "front" money. That is money to finance the picture in its early stages, for 15 to 20 percent of a picture's budget is spent before one ever starts shooting. At that point, a bank is asked to finance the rest of it. Sometimes a bank will put up 60 percent, but generally it refuses to put up more than 50 percent of the required money. If it doesn't figure that a picture is a safe investment, it won't put up any money at all. In making such a decision, the bank studies the outline of the film that is presented, takes into consideration the idea, the treatment, the stars who will appear in it, and so on. Technically speaking, the bank has nothing to do with what goes into a picture, but by being able to loan money or to withhold it, it does have a voice in what goes out of Hollywood.

The situation in the major studios is slightly different, for they usually finance themselves. Occasionally, if they have several unreleased pictures on hand and run short of cash, they can go to the banks and ask for a loan. However, several of the leading banks not only have direct financial interests in the major studios, but have special men assigned to those studios to keep their fingers on the things that are happening.

What does all this mean? Simply that it is high time we stopped thinking of the films in the terms that the publicity writers would have us think, in their frank "selling" campaigns, and began to regard films as a *business,* first, last and always. With that as a basis, we must recognize the fact that if we want the films to do anything for us we must make it unprofitable for them not to do it, and profitable for them to do it. We, and our sympathetic white friends, *must not patronize the films to which we object.* We must write letters to film companies, not only letters of protest, but letters that offer constructive suggestions as to what we *do* want to see in films. We must exercise our rights as consumers. Our newspapers, which have so far carried on a wonderful campaign, must be consistent in this regard. They must not in one column carry just criticism of any certain film and in another—probably more prominent place—print the studio's glamorous news release about the same film. The Negro press is one of the most potent weapons we have and it has so far been almost our only effective weapon. The other weapon is our pocketbooks, the price of admission we pay to see picture shows. When we learn to use that weapon purposefully we will have all the consideration we want in Hollywood.

Supposing now, that the big film executives do come over to our point of view and begin to regard consideration for us as an economic asset. We will still be at a disadvantage because what is wrong with the Negro in films *may* be precisely what's wrong with films in general, that they are unimaginative. The people in studios who actually make the pictures have fallen into clichés which effectively hamper all creative effort. Most of the white people in Hollywood are so accustomed to the Negro stereotype that they don't even know what it is. They see sophisticated, well-dressed colored people day after day, and they are courteous and friendly to them, and yet where the making of a picture is concerned, they all feel that a Negro role has to follow that same old pattern. Sometimes Hollywood isn't vicious; it's just stupid. Too many viewpoints creep in. If someone who earns five thousand dollars a week says something is good, it's good—because naturally a person who earns that much, Hollywood reasons, must be right all the time. . . .

Supposing, however, that Negroes should be employed as, say, authorities on matters concerning their race. In all probability they would be paid for their time, their names would be advertised and their opinions ignored, for in Hollywood's mind, any white man's opinion is superior to that of any Negro, no matter whether the white man be the office boy and the Negro an eminent author, or vice versa. Even among Hollywood's liberals, who are supposedly friendly to Negroes, this same quirk persists. They wish to use only the Negro's name while they do the work, order the Negro's thoughts and actions, and so on.

To illustrate this point, I might add that when it comes to giving others advice, I have been considered an authority on Negro music in Hollywood. But when it comes to the actual work, most of my opinions and my work have been calmly thrown out as not being "authentic." A little more than two years ago I resigned from an all-colored film when the studio music head told me my arrangements were "too good." Negro bands in the Bert Williams period "didn't play that well," he added. I protested that at that time I was playing in Negro bands and that they played better then than they do now. Then the music director said my arrangements were "too polite." He wanted something more erotic to make it more authentic, he declared. So I, a Negro, who have worked for almost thirty years successfully in both the commercial and symphonic fields, am not authentic? I found it hard to believe, and wondered whence stemmed his superior knowledge. I was officially called the "Supervisor of Music" on that film. After my resignation, the head of the music department accused me of being insubordinate. I am sure that this was the first time in history that a *supervisor* was ever insubordinate. . . .

So, in the end, it all returns to the most important aspect of this discussion—the financial part of making films. Hollywood is making some concessions, but is still being cautious about the Negro in films, generally speaking. We, on the other hand, are making strong demands for a bettering of conditions, not only for selfish reasons, but because we know, as the members of every minority group know these days, that America's future depends on good inter-racial understanding.

Will our demands be heeded? It all depends on whether we—*thirteen million* of us—have the strength to boycott those films which are not favorable, even to stay away from all motion picture houses if necessary; whether Negro artists have the courage to starve for a little while longer until we can make definite gains; and whether Negro periodicals will back up their splendid editorials and feature stories with a refusal to carry the studio-inspired "news" which, of course, is not news at all.

Can all of us do this? If we can, we have a chance. If we can't, then the sacrifices made by a few of us are made in vain. It is no good for one colored person to take a stand and to have the film executives know all along that they can go to some other colored person who will fix everything up with the Negro race. If we have only a few Quislings we are licked before we start. If we are unified we can be strong.

from The Crisis of the Negro Intellectual

Harold Cruse

The civil rights movement cannot really give cultural leadership in any effective way—it is too suffused with the compulsion to legitimize its social aims with American standards. The leaders of the civil rights movement, along with all the "civil writers," subordinate themselves to the very cultural values of the white world that are used either to negate, or deny the Negro cultural equality, and to exploit his cultural ingredients and use them *against* him. This is one of the great traps of racial integrationism—one must accept all the values (positive or negative) of the dominant society into which one struggles to integrate. Let us examine two very prominent cultural questions out of the American twentieth-century past and see how they were handled. Both of these are issues of the 1920's that have become institutionalized in today's Americana. One is exemplified by the folk-opera *Porgy and Bess,* a cultural product, the other by Duke Ellington, a cultural personality.

In May, 1959, following the successful opening of *A Raisin in the Sun,* its author Lorraine Hansberry debated Otto Preminger on a television program in Chicago, over what she labeled the deplorable "stereotypes" of *Porgy and Bess.* The film version of the folk opera, directed by Preminger, had just been released and it starred none other than Sidney Poitier, who also headlined Miss Hansberry's play on Broadway. This was, of course, not the first time *Porgy and Bess* had been criticized by Negroes. Ever since its premiere in 1935, it has been under attack from certain Negro quarters because it reveals southern Negroes in an unfavorable light. Hence Miss Hansberry's criticisms were nothing very new or original. What *was* new, however, were the times and the circumstances. Miss Hansberry objected to *Porgy* because stereotypes "constitute bad art" when "the artist hasn't tried hard enough to understand his characters." She claimed that although Gershwin had written a great musical score, he had fallen for what she called the exotic in American culture: "We, over a period of time, have apparently decided that within American life we have one great repository where we're going to focus and imagine sensuality and exaggerated sensuality, all very removed and earthy things—and this great image is the American Negro."

When Preminger asked Miss Hansberry if she suspected the motives of those who had written and produced *Porgy,* she replied: "We cannot afford the luxuries of mistakes of other people. So it isn't a matter of being hostile to you, but on the other hand it's also a matter of never ceasing to try to get you to understand that your mistakes can be painful, even those which come from excellent intentions. We've had great wounds from great intentions."

During this debate there was also injected a discussion of *Carmen Jones*—a white-created, Negro version of the Bizet opera, *Carmen.* Miss Hansberry did not like *Carmen Jones* either; but oddly enough (and also characteristically), she weakened her argument on the subject of artistic integrity by wanting to know why no whites had been cast in this caricature of *Carmen,* as if to imply that interracial casting would have made it more acceptable as art. Behind this query there lurked, of course, the whole muddled question of integration in the arts. Also implicit was the Negro integrationist's main peeve in the theater—the "all-Negro play" (or musical), which they deplore as a symbol of segregation, and the "all-white play," which it is their bounden duty to "integrate," even if the author never had Negroes in mind. Needless to point out, the film *Porgy and Bess* had its Broadway and neighborhood run, and hundreds of working-class Negroes (whom Miss Hansberry claimed she wrote about in *Raisin*), lined up at the box offices to see this colorful film "stereotype" of their people.

This whole episode revealed some glaring facts to substantiate my claim that the Negro creative intellectual does not even approach possession of a positive literary and cultural critique—either of his own art, or that other art created for him by whites. In the first place, Lorraine Hansberry revealed that she knew little about the history of this folk-opera, or how or why it was written. She was only concerned with the fact that it was a stereotype. This already precluded the possibility of Miss Hansberry or anyone rendering the kind of critique *Porgy and Bess* deserves from the Negro point of view. Hence, the whole debate was worthless and a waste of time except from the point of view of making some more noisy, but superficial, integrationist propaganda.

The real cultural issues surrounding *Porgy and Bess,* as it relates to the American Negro presence, have never been confronted by the Negro intelligentsia—inside or outside the theater. The two most obvious points a Negro critic should make are: 1.) that a folk-opera of this genre *should have been written* by Negroes themselves and has not; 2.) that such a folk-opera, even if it *had been written* by Negroes, would never have been supported, glorified and acclaimed, as *Porgy* has, by the white cultural elite of America.

Lorraine Hansberry, taking to the television rostrum on art and culture *à la Negre,* was like a solitary defender, armed with a dull sword, rushing out on a charger to meet a regiment. But once having met an opposing general she immediately capitulates—"My intentions are not really hostile but you all have wounded *us.*" For Miss Hansberry to have criticized *Porgy* merely on content was, of course, her unmitigated privilege; but on this basis, her own play was wide open for some criticism on art and the image of the American Negro, which it never got. To criticize any play today involving Negroes, purely on content, is not enough. Most Negro criticism of *Porgy* has been of middle-class origin, although the Negro middle class has never been at all sympathetic to the realities of southern Negro folk characteristics in any way, shape or form. Hence, a generically class-oriented non-identification was inherent in Miss Hansberry's views.

Porgy and Bess has successfully weathered all such criticisms on its content and has been enshrined in America's rather empty cultural hall of fame as the great American musical classic. It has been shipped all around the world and proudly displayed as America's greatest artistic achievement. How can one really attack America's "greatest artistic achievement," especially when it is about Negroes? *Porgy* is surely the most contradictory cultural symbol ever created in the Western world.

To attack it, one must see it in terms of something more than mere content. It must be criticized from the Negro point of view as the most perfect symbol of the Negro creative artist's cultural denial, degradation, exclusion, exploitation and acceptance of white paternalism. *Porgy and Bess* exemplifies this peculiarly American cultural pathology, most vividly, most historically, and most completely. It combines the problems of Negro theater, music, acting, writing, and even dancing, all in one artistic package, for the Negro has expressed whatever creative originality he can lay claim to, in each of these aspects of art. However, Negroes had no part in writing, directing, producing, or staging this folk-opera about Negroes (unless it was in a strictly subordinate role). In fact, the first recording of *Porgy* used the voices of Lawrence Tibbett and other white singers, because it was not at first believed that Negroes were "good" enough. As a symbol of that deeply-ingrained, American cultural paternalism practiced on Negroes ever since the first Southern white man blacked his face, the folk-opera *Porgy and Bess* should be forever banned by all Negro performers in the United States. No Negro singer, actor, or performer should ever submit to a role in this vehicle again. If white producers want to stage this folk-opera it should be performed by white performers made up in blackface, because it is distorted imitation all the way through. Musically, it is a rather pedestrian blend of imitation-Puccini and imitation-South Carolina-Negro folk music that Gershwin culled. In theme, it presents the "simple black people" just the way white liberal paternalists love to see them. The fact that such Negro types *did* exist is beside the point. Culturally, it is a product of American developments that were intended to shunt Negroes off into a tight box of subcultural, artistic dependence, stunted growth, caricature, aesthetic self-mimicry imposed by others, and creative insolvency.

But the superficial Negro creative intelligentsia, who have become so removed from their meaningful traditions, cannot see things this way, so blindly obsessed are they with the modern mania for instant integration. They do not understand the cultural history of America and where they fit in that historical scheme. They understand next to nothing about the 1920's and how the rather fluid, contending cultural trends among blacks and whites were frozen in that decade, once white control of cultural and creative power patterns was established to the supreme detriment of blacks. They are not aware that the white critics of that time were saying that Negro creative artists were, for the most part, primitives; and that Gilbert Seldes, for example, asserted that Negro musicians and composers were creatively and artistically backward. They are not aware that for critics like Seldes, the Negroes were the anti-intellectual, uninhibited, unsophisticated, intuitive children of jazz music who functioned with aesthetic "emotions" rather than with the disciplined "mind" of white jazzmen. For such critics, the real artists of Negro folk expression were the George Gershwins, the Paul Whitemans and the Cole Porters. Seldes asserted in 1924:

> Nowhere is the failure of the Negro to exploit his gifts more obvious than in the use he had made of the jazz orchestra; for although nearly every Negro jazz band is better than nearly every white band, no Negro band has yet come up to the level of the best white ones, and the leader of the best of all, by a little joke, is called [Paul] Whiteman.

This was a personal opinion, but whether true or false, it typified the white cultural attitudes toward all forms and practices of Negro art: Compared to the Western intellectual standards of art and culture, the Negro does not measure up. Thus every Negro artist, writer, dramatist, poet, composer, musician, *et al,* comes under the guillotine of this cultural judgment. What this judgment really means is that the Negro is artistically, creatively, and culturally inferior; and therefore, all the established social power wielded by the white cultural elite will be used to keep the Negro creative artist in his place. But the historical catch in all this is that the white Protestant Anglo-Saxon in America has nothing in his native American tradition that is aesthetically and culturally original, except that which derives from the Negro presence.

Seldes' mixed feelings and critical ambivalence concerning Negro music stemmed from his awareness that jazz would have to become America's national music, or at least form its basic ingredients. This grievously worried many white critics then, and it explains why they still maintain the artistic superiority of the European symphonic music tradition, refuting that jazz is the basis of the American classical music tradition. From these attitudes on the cultural arts, based on racial values, whites have cultivated their own literary and cultural critique. But it has been a critique predicated on the cultural ideals of a group whose English-North European antecedents have been too culturally ego-ridden, unoriginal, ultra-conservative and desiccated to generate a flourishing national culture. Hence historically, there has been on the cultural front in America a tense ideological war for ethnic identity and ascendancy. This competition has taken on strange and unique patterns. Often it is between WASPs and Jews, but more often than not, it is a collaboration between WASPs and Jews, on high levels, against the Negro. Since it is less possible for the Negro to "pass" for a WASP, than for a member of any other ethnic group, it is the Negro minority who is the most vulnerable and defenseless on the cultural front. In this war of indentity over cultural arts standards, the Negro functions under a double or triple jeopardy: Without a literary and cultural critique of his own, the Negro cannot fight for and maintain a position in the cultural world.

Thus the Hansberry attack on *Porgy and Bess* was almost totally meaningless. Even a total Negro boycott of this film which (theoretically) should have been called, could not have been—for the same reason that Negro actors and performers, led by Sidney Poitier, did not refuse to act in this film in the first place. If the Negro creative intellectuals actually had any real aesthetic standards of their own, Hollywood could not have made this film at all. Since the 1957 boycott by the Montgomery Negroes, showing what kind of sacrifices are necessary when it comes to a principle, every Negro—high or low, rich or poor—has the moral obligation at all times to give up immediate comforts and privileges for long-range objectives.

Black Movies

Charles Michener
(*Newsweek,* October 23, 1972)

Moral: A Baadasssss Nigger Is Coming Back To Collect Some Dues.
—Postscript to Melvin Van Peebles's film, "Sweet Sweetback's Baadasssss Song"

What Van Peebles warned has come to pass. All over the country, "bad-ass niggers" are collecting dues with a vengeance—and, if you don't believe it, just head downtown for a movie. Outside the old silver-screen palaces on New York's Times Square, along Chicago's Loop, in downtown Detroit, the crowds are young, mostly black and bigger than they've been since Scarlett O'Hara ran off with Rhett Butler. Inside, the furious action on celluloid is pointed toward the triumph of black good over white evil; audiences are whooping it up with such glee that projectionists must jack up the volume during the climaxes, and theater owners are counting more dollars than they've handled in years. The black-movie explosion is on—and the controversial fallout is just beginning to settle.

Van Peebles set it off—and set the tone—when he vowed more than two years ago to "get the Man's foot out of all our black asses" by making a film "about a brother *getting* the Man's foot out of his ass." The result was the gritty, profane "Sweetback," a mythic opus about a black stud's successful revolt against white society, which grossed $11 million—an amazing success for a movie made and distributed completely outside established industry channels. A couple of months later, Gordon Parks came out with the equally low-budget "Shaft," about a black private eye, which by year's end had racked up $12 million in North America and singlehandedly rescued M-G-M from near financial ruin.

Never slow to read handwriting that's punctuated with dollar signs, Hollywood quickly took note of two facts: first, whites had begun to flee the inner cities, vacating many big downtown theaters and leaving a vacuum for the burgeoning number of black moviegoers to fill; second, blacks would turn out in far greater numbers for films that featured black heroes and heroines and plenty of sex and violence than they would for white adventure flicks. In short order, the studio bosses began restocking—and revamping—their arsenals.

Talented black actors, directors and writers were suddenly plucked out of studio back rooms, modeling agencies and ghetto theaters, and turned loose on new black projects. White heroes of scripts that had been lying on the shelf were instantly converted into black heroes and sent scurrying before the cameras. Much of the white trash emerged as black trash and was quickly buried after release. But an astonishing number of black films have been paying off at a rate to put their white counterparts in the shade—and in the process have not only produced the first gold mine in years for a struggling industry, but also have split the U.S. black community into those who justify or at least discriminate among the films, and those for whom the entire phenomenon is a violent blow to black dignity and social well-being.

Of this year's Westerns, the two biggest nuggets are black—"Buck and the Preacher" ($9 million gross so far), in which Sidney Poitier and Harry Belafonte lead ex-slaves to a new life in the West, and "The Legend of Nigger Charley" ($5 million), in which ex-pro football star Fred Williamson goes from slavery to gunfighting. Tops in the action genre are "Shaft's" sequel, "Shaft's Big Score" ($10 million), which again features Richard Roundtree as the supercool John Shaft, foiling a gang of white hoods; "Melinda" ($5 million), with Calvin

From the motion picture *Shaft's Big Score.* Courtesy of Films Inc.—MGM.

Lockhart as a Los Angeles disk jockey wiping out white gangsters who have murdered his girl friend; "Cool Breeze," a black remake of "The Asphalt Jungle"; "Slaughter," with Jim Brown also doing in the mob; and the just-released "Hammer," with Fred Williamson, using his old football nickname, as a boxer who won't go crooked.

A Potential Explosiveness

American International Pictures has a bonanza in the first all-black vampire movie—"Blacula," which turns America's favorite Transylvanian bloodsucker into an accursed ex-African prince. And "Come Back Charleston Blue," the sequel to 1970's "Cotton Comes to Harlem," has already pulled in $7 million with the antics of Godfrey Cambridge and Raymond St. Jacques as Harlem cops who destroy a black dope lord. Finally, there's "Super Fly," directed by Gordon Parks Jr., which in a little more than two months is up to $11 million and is currently outgrossing every other movie on the market—black or white—with its offbeat tale of a black cocaine pusher (Ron O'Neal) who not only beats the system—both the mob and the cops—but gets out with a cool half-million.

All this is only the beginning. On their way in the next four months are Van Peebles's film of his Broadway musical play, "Don't Play Us Cheap," a biography of Billie Holiday, "Lady Sings the Blues," starring Diana Ross, and a score of entertainments with titles like "Blackenstein," "Black Gun," "Black Majesty," "Blackfather," "Black Christ" and "The Werewolf From Watts" as well as "Hit Man," "The Book of Numbers," "Trick Baby" and "Cleopatra Jones." In an industry that has recently been producing little more than 200 films a year, fully one-fourth of those now in the planning stage are black.

A long overdue avenue to success for black talent and a kick for hungry black moviegoers, the phenomenon has nonetheless drawn considerable fire from many black intellectuals, political leaders and laymen who are mounting protests against the industry and picketing theaters for showing the allegedly pro-drug "Super Fly."

Many of the talented blacks who are involved in making these movies are torn between conflicting attitudes about their value and significance. Robert Hooks is a leading black actor, a co-founder and director of the outstanding Negro Ensemble Company in New York who is currently organizing the D.C. Black Repertory Company in predominantly black Washington. Like other serious actors, such as Calvin Lockhart, Rosalind Cash and William Marshall, Hooks is ambivalent about his participation in the black-movie explosion. In the forthcoming "Trouble Man," he plays T, a ghetto hustler who's hired, like a fast-sword samurai in a Japanese Western, to settle the rivalry between two racket gangs in Los Angeles. "The only interesting subject left for the American stage or screen is the black man," says Hooks. "So these producers have obviously found a good thing to make money on. But for the most part they have been doing these films in bad taste."

Charges of "Treason"

There is no such ambivalence in the attitude of black community leaders such as Junius Griffin, head of the Beverly Hills–Hollywood branch of the NAACP. Says the angry Griffin: "We must insist that our children are not exposed to a steady diet of so-called black movies that glorify black males as pimps, dope pushers, gangsters and super males with vast physical prowess but no cognitive skills." The danger of this fantasy, adds black critic Clayton Riley, is "to reinforce the ordinary black human being's sense of personal helplessness and inadequacy."

Black Panther chieftain Huey Newton finds the films dangerously counter-revolutionary (though he exempts "Sweetback" and "Buck and the Preacher"): "They leave revolution out or, if it's in, they make it look stupid and naive. I think it's part of a conspiracy." And Tony Brown, dean of Howard University's school of communications and producer of educational television's "Black Journal," lays the blame squarely with the blacks themselves. "The blaxploitation films," he says, "are a phenomenon of self-hate. Look at the image of 'Super Fly.' Going to see yourself as a drug dealer when you're oppressed is sick. Not only are blacks identifying with him, they're paying for the identification. It's sort of like a Jew paying to get into Auschwitz." Those blacks who contribute to the making of these films, adds Brown, no matter how they rationalize it, are guilty of nothing less than "treason."

Vigorous Defense

But those involved with the black films countercharge that the critics are obtuse, overwrought and condescending to their own people. "It's ridiculous," says Gordon Parks, "to imply that blacks don't know the difference between truth and fantasy and therefore will be influenced by these films in an unhealthy way. I knew a black preacher in Chicago and I remember people who wanted to kill their white bosses coming to the prayer meeting and being calmed down by the preacher. These movies are serving the same therapeutic function."

Ron O'Neal, who plays Priest, the victorious pusher in "Super Fly," argues that the film's critics are simply out of touch. "The plot is so old hat to every kid in Harlem," he says. "Blacks are no longer interested in perpetuating the old myths. The critics of 'Super Fly' want to support the myth that crime doesn't pay. But we all happen to know that crime *is* paying off for some people every day." And James Earl Jones, who plays the first black President in "The Man," says: "If they're going to put the damper on John Shaft let them put it on John Wayne too and they'll find out that there are a lot of people who need those fantasies."

Ex-footballers Jim Brown and Fred Williamson claim that they are doing no more on screen than they did on the gridiron—and, for that matter, no more than white screen heroes have been doing all along. "Where were the black critics when Cagney, Bogart and Raft were doing their thing?" growls Williamson. "When I was a kid, I played Hopalong Cassidy and nobody hit me in the mouth and said, 'Don't be that way'."

When Williamson was a kid, of course, there were no black Hopalongs to imitate. Black movies had been around since the early talkies (King Vidor's 1929

"Hallelujah" was the first distinguished all-sound film) but until recently, the black image on screen ran through a short spectrum from the shuffling Stepin Fetchit, on the one hand, to the noble but amenable Sidney Poitier on the other—both outsiders in an alien society they were bound to accept, both fully acceptable to white sensibilities. Now the tables are turned. In the world of the new black film, the white man is the outsider—and rarely is he acceptable to black sensibilities.

Hot off the Streets

Unlike most white escapist fare with its never-never landscapes of purple sage and alpine luxury, the strongest of the new black films are firmly rooted in the audience's own backyards—"Super Fly," "Charleston Blue" and "Shaft" in the squalid, decayed slums of Harlem, "Melinda" in barren, bleached-out Watts. The spectacular Eldorado Cadillac driven by Priest in "Super Fly" gets quick recognition from some of the Harlem members of the audience because it actually belongs to "K.C.", a well-known Harlem pimp who plays himself in the film.

It is hard to gauge the true influence of these movies, especially on young blacks. The newest rage among black youths at one Los Angeles high school is to wear their hair straightened and flowing, to sport wide-lapeled midi coats and to adorn themselves with tiny silver crosses and "coke spoons" around their necks—all à la Priest in "Super Fly." But more important than clothes or hair is the "super bad" appeal of these movies. But there is more involved than that. Gordon Stulberg, the much-respected head of Twentieth Century-Fox , believes that "black films give blacks much more opportunity to feel vicariously in control of their environment than whites get from James Bond movies." And, indeed, control is first among virtues in these movies: grace under pressure (whether in bed or in the precinct house), mastery of self-defense (by karate or judo) and, above all, a hatred for heroin—the main tool of oppression and self-oppression.

At bottom, though, the black films may have more of a political dimension than any of the militant critics suspect. For with the exception of Jim Brown, whose prepotent Slaughter is the only black in an all-white world, the new black heroes are not odd men out in the white tradition of Cagney, Bogart and John Garfield, but odd men in—who only venture out of their close-knit black community to become invincible guerrillas in the white community.

Black outspokenness about the content of their studio-controlled films is on the increase—and already there have been several notable victories. It was at actor William Marshall's insistence that his role of Blacula was changed from that of a black American paying a social visit to Transylvania to that of an African prince seeking an end to the slave trade—before he falls into the clutches of Dracula. In playing the clap-trappy part, says his co-star Vonetta McGee, "Marshall gave so much dignity that you're crying for him in the end."

From the motion picture **Super Fly.** Copyright © 1972 by Warner Bros.—Seven Arts Inc.

Fighting for Human Elements

Hired to direct Twentieth's "Trouble Man," Ivan Dixon discovered that the script had the leading black female character, played by Paula Kelly, jumping in and out of bed like a cat in heat, and called the NAACP in to negotiate a change. And three of the most outspoken black talents around—director Hugh Robertson, writer Lonne Elder III and actress Rosalind Cash—took one look at M-G-M's original script for "Melinda" and plunged into a battle that ended with the conversion of hopeless trash into stylish and diverting trash.

"I had to fight and fight for any human elements in the story," recalls Robertson, who previously had edited "Shaft." "They kept pushing for all sex and violence. I had to insist on the dinner scene between Melinda (Vonetta McGee) and Frankie (Calvin Lockhart) so we could see some kind of relationship between them, not just bring her into the story and suddenly have her dead the next morning. And I had to fight to keep a scene between Frankie and Terry (Rosalind Cash) that shows her as a black woman who's strong and a real person."

Says Cash, a fine stage actress: "I'm proud of what I did with Terry. When I go up to Harlem, the hard-working soul sisters come up to me and say, 'You were for real in that part; I know what that character was all about'." And Elder, who wrote the prize-winning play "Ceremonies in Dark Old Men," sums up his Hollywood experience in general by recalling what one big studio executive once said to him: "They want s–– and we're giving them s––."

It's that kind of exploitative—and racist—attitude that has so many veteran black activists up in arms, and, to combat it with more than words, they are trying to apply various kinds of pressure to the movie industry. Some of them have rallied to the idea that black films can be used as wedges to make, as one puts it, "the industry pay its dues to the black community"—in money. In Seattle, black owners of a black neighborhood theater have brought suit against a white-owned organization, claiming the right to share in the first-run distribution of "Super Fly." New York militants have made Harlem virtually out-of-bounds to major filmmakers with a variety of demands, ranging from an increased proportion of blacks on shooting crews to direct payments to "community organizations."

Still other activists are batting around such ideas as a separate rating system for black movies and a black review board to screen scripts before production. Internal bickering has prevented members of the newly formed Coalition Against Blaxploitation in Los Angeles from doing anything with these hot potatoes—out of mindfulness, perhaps, of Jim Brown's fierce admonition: "That's like being under Hitler. I don't want a black or a white Hitler."

Plausible or not, such pressures are having their effect on white movie moguls. M-G-M's president, James Aubrey, pointedly refused to grant *Newsweek* an interview, leaving the impression that he wanted to lie low until all the controversy had blown over. According to actor Raymond St. Jacques, one group of executives decided to do a black film, then nervously converted all the characters into Puerto Ricans.

As Brown and several other blacks with clout see it, the key to better black films—and bigger payoff to blacks—is to get wealthy blacks involved in the capitalization of new films, just as two black dentists were in the financing of "Super Fly." "We're allowing white producers to make money off us in our major market like we've done through the years," says Brown. "We've got the capital if blacks would only give it up." Recently, Roy Innes, director of CORE, announced that his organization intended to enter the business, but the where-withal to do so has not yet appeared. Jesse Jackson of Operation PUSH (People United to Save Humanity) has expressed hopes of organizing black artists, writers and producers into a cooperative film venture. And Robert Hooks is shaping up "Nation Time Productions," to produce worthwhile material in films, TV, theater and music, using outstanding black talent and money—a project that could amount, he says, "to a black economic revolution in the entertainment industry."

Breaking Out of the Groove

Perhaps the most hopeful portent for better black movies is the almost uniform desire of the new black pantheon of directors, writers and stars to break out of the sex-and-violence bag. "Unless black films explore other areas of black experience," warns "Melinda's" superhero Calvin Lockhart, "black films will wind up on the shelf and eventually stop." Sick of films like "Shaft," Gordon Parks has refused to oversee any more sequels (five more are planned). And rather than doing a sequel to their "Super Fly," his director son, Gordon Jr., and screenwriter Phillip Fenty are working on a project which, says Fenty, is "totally removed from drugs." Roundtree himself, the ex-model who is perhaps the reigning black superstar, sums up a widespread feeling among his colleagues: "What we want in our movies from now on is to show black people winning because they use their heads, not because they do violence with their hands."

But in the end, it is economics—not good intentions—that will decide the future of black movies. And at the moment, nearly everyone in the business sees the great black hope embodied in a moving little film called "Sounder." Directed by a white veteran, Martin Ritt, and scripted by Elder, "Sounder" stands apart from the prevailing tide in several important respects: its documentary feel for the historical context of American black experience; its lack of shrillness about white bigotry; its elevation of a black woman as played by Cicely Tyson into a complex, forceful human, not a groovy sex object, and, most of all, its quiet, almost mythical tale about a family of Louisiana sharecroppers in the Depression who, in Faulkner's famous words, not only endure but prevail.

But will "Sounder" prevail? Even here blacks are split: some, like actress Tyson and *Newsweek*'s Los Angeles bureau chief, John Dotson, seeing hope in the film's quiet dignity; others smelling ripoff in those very qualities. "Sounder," says one black actor, "was made for whites who want to believe that blacks are full of love and trust and patience. It avoids dealing with things like rage and bitterness and the need for some kind of release. That kind of people don't survive here on the streets of New York. I took a girl to see 'Sounder' who used to do laundry for white people. She wasn't going to be entertained by a film about black suffering, because she *knows* about black suffering." Replies Miss Tyson: "I think we have come far enough to look back on our lives with pride. It's because of people like those in 'Sounder' that we've come as far as we have."

In any case, the black is no longer a bit player on the American movie screen. "Just as we've done with theater and music," Ron O'Neal says, "black people will develop a new art form of movies in this country—given the time and opportunity."

FOR DISCUSSION

1.   In this section of the book there are a few proposed solutions for overcoming the one-dimensional portrayal of Blacks on the screen. Which of these proposals do you think might work best and why? Can you offer any alternative solutions to the problem of stereotyped casting?

2.   Authors Harold Cruse and William Grant Still cite that a basic cause for the problem of stereotyped images is the general low esteem held by White film-makers for Black creative talent. Considering such an attitude exists behind the scenes, is it any wonder that Blacks have been portrayed as they have? Do you feel that Cruse's solution, the creation of a totally Black "cultural identity," is a feasible one? Do you agree with his blaming the Black artists who cooperated with the White manipulation of them, particularly in so-called "Negro-genre" pieces like *Porgy and Bess?*

PART SIX

The Movie Indian
and the Movie Jew—
Parallel Studies in Stereotyping

Blacks, of course, have not been the only minority group which the movies has stereotyped. The Jews, the Irish, the Italians (remember the protests against television's *The Untouchables*), the Greeks, the Chinese, the American Indian, and just about any other ethnic and racial minority you can name have often been demeaned and dehumanized on the screen. In this section two interpretations of non-Black stereotyping are presented to demonstrate the depth of the problem, and to contrast the Black experience.

Vine Deloria, Jr.'s two powerful books—*Custer Died for Your Sins* and *We Talk, You Listen*—have become known as the angry "Indian manifesto." Deloria, who is a full-blooded Sioux, examines the nature of "stock" Indian roles on the screen and discusses the harm they do. His conclusions are an interesting comment on the psychological problems of a society which believes in stereotypes.

Writer Gary Carey, in his article from *The National Jewish Monthly,* traces the history of the Jewish portrayal in the movies and cites several parallels to the images of other groups who've been stereotyped. Carey's article is particularly interesting in its comments on the large numbers of Jewish film producers who helped give birth to the stereotype by insisting on a favorable image for Jews. Apparently, this was more important than a human, realistic portrayal.

Stereotyping

Vine Deloria, Jr.

(from *We Talk, You Listen*)

One reason that Indian people have not been heard from until recently is that we have been completely covered up by movie Indians. Western movies have been such favorites that they have dominated the public's conception of what Indians are. It is not all bad when one thinks about the handsome Jay Silverheels bailing the Lone Ranger out of a jam, or Ed Ames rescuing Daniel Boone with some clever Indian trick. But the other mythologies that have wafted skyward because of the movies have blocked out any idea that there might be real Indians with real problems.

Other minority groups have fought tenaciously against stereotyping, and generally they have been successful. Italians quickly quashed the image of them as mobsters that television projected in *The Untouchables.* Blacks have been successful in getting a more realistic picture of the black man in a contemporary setting because they have had standout performers like Bill Cosby and Sidney Poitier to represent them.

Since stereotyping was highlighted by motion pictures, it would probably be well to review the images of minority groups projected in the movies in order to understand how the situation looks at present. Perhaps the first aspect of stereotyping was the tendency to exclude people on the basis of their inability to handle the English language. Not only were racial minorities excluded, but immigrants arriving on these shores were soon whipped into shape by ridicule of their English.

Traditional stereotypes pictured the black as a happy watermelon-eating darky whose sole contribution to American society was his indiscriminate substitution of the "d" sound for "th." Thus a black always said "dis" and "dat," as in "lift dat bale." The "d" sound carried over and was used by white gangsters to indicate disfavor with their situation, as in "dis is de end, ya rat." The important thing was to indicate that blacks were like lisping children not yet competent to undertake the rigors of economic opportunities and voting.

Mexicans were generally portrayed as shiftless and padded out for siesta, without any redeeming qualities whatsoever. Where the black had been handicapped by his use of the "d," the Mexican suffered from the use of the double "e." This marked them off as a group worth watching. Mexicans, according to the stereotype, always said "theenk," "peenk," and later "feenk." Many advertisements today still continue this stereotype, thinking that it is cute and cuddly.

These groups were much better off than Indians were. Indians were always devoid of any English whatsoever. They were only allowed to speak when an important message had to be transmitted on the screen. For example, "many pony soliders die" was meant to indicate that Indians were going to attack the peaceful settlers who happened to have broken their three hundredth treaty moments before. Other than that Indian linguistic ability was limited to "ugh" and "kemo sabe" (which means honky in some obscure Indian language).

The next step was to acknowledge that there was a great American dream to which any child could aspire. (It was almost like the train in the night that Richard Nixon heard as a child anticipating the dream fairy.) The great American dream was projected in the early World War II movies. The last reel was devoted to a stirring proclamation that we were going to win the war and it showed factories producing airplanes, people building ships, and men marching in uniform to the transports. There was a quick pan of a black face before the scene shifted to scenes of orchards, rivers, Mount Rushmore, and the Liberty Bell as we found out what we were fighting for.

The new images expressed a profound inability to understand why minority groups couldn't "make it" when everybody knew what America was all about—freedom and equality. By projecting an image of everyone working hard to win the war, the doctrine was spread that America was just one big happy family and that there really weren't any differences so long as we had to win the war.

It was a rare war movie in the 1940s that actually showed a black or a Mexican as a bona fide fighting man. When they did appear it was in the role of cooks or orderlies serving whites. In most cases this was a fairly accurate statement of their situation, particularly with respect to the Navy.

World War II movies were entirely different for Indians. Each platoon of red-blooded white American boys was equipped with its own set of Indians. When the platoon got into trouble and was surrounded, its communications cut off except for one slender line to regimental headquarters, and that line tapped by myriads of Germans, Japanese, or Italians, the stage was set for the dramatic episode of the Indians.

John Wayne, Randolph Scott, Sonny Tufts, or Tyrone Power would smile broadly as he played his ace, which until this time had been hidden from view. From nowhere, a Navajo, Comanche, Cherokee, or Sioux would appear, take the telephone, and in some short and inscrutable phraseology communicate such a plenitude of knowledge to his fellow tribesman (fortunately situated at the general's right hand) that fighting units thousands of miles away would instantly perceive the situation and rescue the platoon. The Indian would disappear as mysteriously as he had come, only to reappear the next week in a different battle to perform his esoteric rites. Anyone watching war movies during the 40s would have been convinced that without Indian telephone operators the war would have been lost irretrievably, in spite of John Wayne.

Indians were America's secret weapon against the forces of evil. The typing spoke of a primitive gimmick, and it was the strangeness of Indians that made them visible, not their humanity. With the Korean War era and movies made during the middle 50s, other minority groups began to appear and Indians were pushed into the background. This era was the heyday of the "All-American Platoon." It was the ultimate conception of intergroup relations. The "All-American Platoon" was a "one each": one black, one Mexican, one Indian, one farm boy from Iowa, one Southerner who hated blacks, one boy from Brooklyn, one Polish boy from the urban slums of the Midwest, one Jewish intellectual, and one college boy. Every possible stereotype was included and it resulted in a portrayal of Indians as another species of human being for the first time in moving pictures.

The platoon was always commanded by a veteran of grizzled countenance who had been at every battle in which the United States had ever engaged. The whole story consisted in killing off the members of the platoon until only the veteran and the college boy were left. The Southerner and the black would die in each other's arms singing "Dixie." The Jewish intellectual and the Indian formed some kind of attachment and were curiously the last ones killed. When the smoke cleared, the college boy, with a prestige wound in the shoulder, returned to his girl, and the veteran reconciled with his wife and checked out another platoon in anticipation of taking the same hill in the next movie.

While other groups have managed to make great strides since those days, Indians have remained the primitive unknown quantity. Dialogue has reverted back to the monosyllabic grunt and even pictures that attempt to present the Indian side of the story depend upon unintelligible noises to present their

From the motion picture *Shalako*. Courtesy of Films Inc.—Cinerama.

message. The only exception to this rule is a line famed for its durability over the years. If you fall asleep during the Late Show and suddenly awaken to the words "go in peace my son," it is either an Indian chief bidding his son good-bye as the boy heads for college or a Roman Catholic priest forgiving Paul Newman or Steve McQueen for killing a hundred men in the preceding reel.

Anyone raising questions about the image of minority groups as portrayed in television and the movies is automatically suspect as an un-American and subversive influence on the minds of the young. The historical, linguistic, and cultural differences are neatly blocked out by the fad of portraying members of minority groups in roles which formerly were reserved for whites. Thus Burt Reynolds played a Mohawk detective busy solving the crime problem in New York City. Diahann Carroll played a well-to-do black widow with small child in a television series that was obviously patterned after the unique single-headed white family.

In recent years the documentary has arisen to present the story of Indian people and a number of series on Black America have been produced. Indian documentaries are singularly the same. A reporter and television crew hasten to either the Navajo or Pine Ridge reservation, quickly shoot reels on poverty conditions, and return East blithely thinking that they have captured the essence of Indian life. In spite of the best intentions, the eternal yearning to present an exciting story of a strange people overcomes, and the endless cycle of poverty-oriented films continues.

This type of approach continually categorizes the Indian as an incompetent boob who can't seem to get along and who is hopelessly mired in a poverty of his own making. Hidden beneath these documentaries is the message that Indians really WANT to live this way. No one has yet filmed the incredible progress that is being made by the Makah tribe, the Quinaults, Red Lake Chippewas, Gila River Pima-Maricopas, and others. Documentaries project the feeling that reservations should be eliminated because the conditions are so bad. There is no effort to present the bright side of Indian life.

With the rise of ethnic studies programs and courses in minority-group history, the situation has become worse. People who support these programs assume that by communicating the best aspects of a group they have somehow solved the major problems of that group in its relations with the rest of society. By emphasizing that black is beautiful or that Indians have contributed the names of rivers to the road map, many people feel that they have done justice to the group concerned.

One theory of interpretation of Indian history that has arisen in the past several years is that all of the Indian war chiefs were patriots defending their lands. This is the "patriot chief" interpretation of history. Fundamentally it is a good theory in that it places a more equal balance to interpreting certain Indian wars as wars of resistance. It gets away from the tendency, seen earlier in this century, to classify all Indian warriors as renegades. But there is a tendency to overlook the obvious renegades, Indians who were treacherous and would have been renegades had there been no whites to fight. The patriot chiefs interpretation also conveniently overlooks the fact that every significant leader of the previous century was eventually done in by his own people in one way or another. Sitting Bull was killed by Indian police working for the government. Geronimo was captured by an army led by Apache scouts who sided with the United States.

If the weak points of each minority group's history are to be covered over by a sweetness-and-light interpretation based on what we would like to think happened rather than what did happen, we doom ourselves to decades of further racial strife. Most of the study programs today emphasize the goodness that is inherent in the different minority communities, instead of trying to present a balanced story. There are basically two schools of interpretation running through all of these efforts as the demand for black, red, and brown pride dominates the programs.

One theory derives from the "All-American Platoon" concept of a decade ago. Under this theory members of the respective racial minority groups had an important role in the great events of American history. Crispus Attucks, a black, almost single-handedly started the Revolutionary War, while Eli Parker, the Seneca Indian general, won the Civil War and would have concluded it sooner had not there been so many stupid whites abroad in those days. This is the "cameo" theory of history. It takes a basic "manifest destiny" white interpretation of history and lovingly plugs a few feathers, woolly heads, and sombreros into the famous events of American history. No one tries to explain what an Indian is who was helping the whites destroy his own people, since we are now all Americans and have these great events in common.

The absurdity of the cameo school of ethnic pride is self-apparent. Little Mexican children are taught that there were some good Mexicans at the Alamo. They can therefore be happy that Mexicans have been involved in the significant events of Texas history. Little is said about the Mexicans on the other side at the Alamo. The result is a denial of a substantial Mexican heritage by creating the feeling that "we all did it together." If this trend continues I would not be surprised to discover that Columbus had a Cherokee on board when he set sail from Spain in search of the Indies.

The cameo school smothers any differences that existed historically by presenting a history in which all groups have participated through representatives. Regardless of Crispus Attucks' valiant behavior during the Revolution, it is doubtful that he envisioned another century of slavery for blacks as a cause worth defending.

The other basic school of interpretation is a projection backward of the material blessings of the white middle class. It seeks to identify where all the material wealth originated and finds that each minority group *contributed* something. It can therefore be called the contribution school. Under this conception we should all love Indians because they contributed corn, squash, potatoes, tobacco, coffee, rubber, and other agricultural products. In like manner, blacks and Mexicans are credited with Carver's work on the peanut, blood transfusion, and tacos and tamales.

The ludicrous implication of the contribution school visualizes the minority groups clamoring to enter American society, lined up with an abundance of foods and fancies, presenting them to whites in a never-ending stream of generosity. If the different minority groups were given an overriding 2 percent royalty on their contributions, the same way whites have managed to give themselves royalties for their inventions, this school would have a more realistic impact on minority groups.

The danger with both of these types of ethnic studies is that they present an unrealistic account of the role of minority groups in American history. Certainly there is more to the story of the American Indian than providing cocoa and popcorn for Columbus' landing party. When the clashes of history are smoothed over in favor of a mushy togetherness feeling, then people begin to wonder what has happened in the recent past that has created the conditions of today. It has been the feeling of younger people that contemporary problems have arisen because community leadership has been consistently betraying them. Older statesmen are called Uncle Toms, and the entire fabric of accumulated wisdom and experience of the older generation of minority groups is destroyed.

Rising against the simplistic cameo and contribution schools is the contemporary desire by church leaders to make Christianity relevant to minority groups by transposing the entire Christian myth and archetypes into Indian, black, and Mexican terms. Thus Father Groppi, noted white-black priest, wants to have black churches show a black Christ. This is absurd, because Christ was, as everyone knows, a Presbyterian, and he was a white man. That is to say, for nearly two thousand years he has been a white man. To suddenly show him as black, Mexican, or Indian takes away the whole meaning of the myth.

The Indian counterpart of the black Christ is the Christmas card portraying the Holy Family living in a hogan in Monument Valley on the Navajo reservation. As the shepherds sing and gather their flocks, little groups of Navajo angels announce the birth of the Christchild. The scene is totally patronizing and unrealistic. If the Christchild was born on the Navajo reservation, his chances of surviving the first two years of life would be less than those of the original Jesus with Herod chasing him. (We have not yet reached the point of showing three officials from the Bureau of Indian Affairs coming up the canyon as the Three Wise Men, but someone with a keen sense of relevancy will try it sooner or later.)

This type of religious paternalism overlooks the fact that the original figures of religious myths were designed to communicate doctrines. It satisfies itself by presenting its basic figures as so universalized that anyone can participate at any time in history. Thus the religion that it is trying to communicate becomes ahistorical, as Mickey Mouse and Snow White are ahistorical.

If the attempted renovation of religious imagery is ever combined with the dominant schools of ethnic studies, the result will be the Last Supper as the gathering of the "All-American Platoon" highlighted by the contributions of each group represented. Instead of simple bread and wine the table will be overflowing with pizza, tamales, greens, peanuts, popcorn, German sausage, and hamburgers. Everyone will feel that they have had a part in the creation of the great American Christian social order. Godless Communism will be vanquished.

Under present conceptions of ethnic studies there can be no lasting benefit either to minority groups or to society at large. The pride that can be built into children and youth by acknowledgment of the validity of their group certainly cannot be built by simply transferring symbols and interpretations arising in white cultural history into an Indian, black, or Mexican setting. The result will be to make the minority groups bear the white man's burden by using his symbols and stereotypes as if they were their own.

There must be a drive within each minority group to understand its own uniqueness. This can only be done by examining what experiences were relevant to the group, not what experiences of white America the group wishes itself to be represented in. As an example, the discovery of gold in California was a significant event in the experience of white America. The discovery itself was irrelevant to the western Indian tribes, but the migrations caused by the discovery of gold were vitally important. The two histories can dovetail around this topic but ultimately each interpretation must depend upon its orientation to the group involved.

What has been important and continues to be important is the Constitution of the United States and its continual adaptation to contemporary situations. With the Constitution as a framework and reference point, it would appear that a number of conflicting interpretations of the experience of America could be validly given. While they might conflict at every point as each group defines to its own satisfaction what its experience has meant, recognition that within the Constitutional framework we are engaged in a living process of intergroup relationships would mean that no one group could define the meaning of American society to the exclusion of any other.

Self-awareness of each group must define a series of histories about the American experience. Manifest destiny has dominated thinking in the past because it has had an abstract quality that appeared to interpret experiences accurately. Nearly every racial and ethnic group has had to bow down before this conception of history and conform to an understanding of the world that it did not ultimately believe. Martin Luther King, Jr., spoke to his people on the basis of self-awareness the night before he died. He told them that they as a people would reach the promised land. Without the same sense of destiny, minority groups will simply be adopting the outmoded forms of stereotyping by which whites have deluded themselves for centuries.

We can survive as a society if we reject the conquest-oriented interpretation of the Constitution. While some Indian nationalists want the whole country back, a guarantee of adequate protection of existing treaty rights would provide a meaningful compromise. The Constitution should provide a sense of balance between groups as it has between conflicting desires of individuals.

As each group defines the ideas and doctrines necessary to maintain its own sense of dignity and identity, similarities in goals can be drawn that will have relevance beyond immediate group aspirations. Stereotyping will change radically because the ideological basis for portraying the members of any group will depend on that group's values. Plots in books and movies will have to show life as it is seen from within the group. Society will become broader and more cosmopolitan as innovative themes are presented to it. The universal sense of inhumanity will take on an aspect of concreteness. From the variety of cultural behavior patterns we can devise a new understanding of humanity.

The problem of stereotyping is not so much a racial problem as it is a problem of limited knowledge and perspective. Even though minority groups have suffered in the past by ridiculous characterizations of themselves by white society, they must not fall into the same trap by simply reversing the process that has stereotyped them. Minority groups must thrust through the rhetorical blockade by creating within themselves a sense of "peoplehood." This ultimately means the creation of a new history and not mere amendments to the historical interpretations of white America.

The Long, Long Road
to Brenda Patimkin

Gary Carey

(*The National Jewish Monthly,* October 1971)

"It is not an accident but rather a phase of screen evolution which finds the American motion picture industry, and therefore the screens of the world, administered rather largely by our best and most facile internationalists, the Jews. ... This development has come by the same process and for many of the same reasons as the prior but similar evolution in the garment trade.... The most casual attention will discover that the motion picture and the garment trade have a psychology in common to a marked degree."

This statement, written in 1926 by a film historian, pointed up, perhaps indelicately, two interwoven facts that directly influenced the portrayal of Jews on the screen. The most influential men in American film—the Louis B. Mayers, Samuel Goldwyns, David O. Selznicks, Irving Thalbergs, Harry Cohns, Jesse

Laskys, Carl Laemmles, Darryl Zanucks, the brothers Warner and other studio heads and powerful producers–have been, by a sizable majority, Jewish. Consequently, there was always on the production end a vested interest in the treatment of Jews on the screen. The screen portraits of other minority groups–Negroes, Orientals, Italians–were not always so kindly drawn. Still, the Hollywood industry, when pushed to the wall, was led by businessmen first; what really counted was what showed up on the balance sheet. The principle was generally reflected in their product.

The audiences for the first little films which appeared between the mid-1890s and 1910 were composed largely of immigrants, many of whom could not yet speak English; they adjusted easily to the pantomime of the silent film. Jews went to the nickelodeons in numbers large enough for their patronage to be weighed and courted. An advertisement for a 1908 film, *A Man's Man,* promised a portrait of a Jew different from "stage Jew"; he was not to be burlesqued as in stage melodramas but shown as a character with "manhood, sentiment and convictions." When a film did fall back on the then typical stage portrayal of the villainous Jew there was much hue and cry, as was the case when D. W. Griffith's *The Usurer* appeared in 1919. Griffith did not specifically label the central character as Jewish but audiences so identified him and resented a scene showing the usurer enjoying a luxurious dinner while collectors were out repossessing his victims.

By and large, however, most of the earliest films, when portraying the Jew, did so with great sympathy, although precise assessments are near-impossible since few prints of these films still exist. This was also before the advent of regular film reviewing (which began about 1916) and we do not have the benefit of their second-hand reports. But motion picture trade periodicals of that time often included plot synopses of current films and from these one gets an idea of their general tenor.

Some examples: in *The Airship* (1909), a "Hebrew" with an airship of his own invention takes flight, crashes into the sea, is swallowed by a whale but is rescued by sailors whom he rewards by dancing a hornpipe; in *Cohen's Generosity* (1910), a Jewish pawnshop owner is rescued by a Christian youth from a group of rowdies and repays the debt by rescuing the Christian from penury; in *The Blood of the Poor* (1910), a poor Jewish tailor avoids eviction by allowing his daughter to become a servant in the home of the landlord, where she is seduced while her father dies of starvation and overwork; in *Faith of the Fathers* (1913), a beautiful Jewish girl is torn between her father and her love for a non-Jew; in *The Heart of a Jewess* (1913), a poor girl whose sweatshop earnings have financed the passage of her sweetheart to the New World loses him to another woman; in *The Jew's Christmas* (1913), a rabbi disowns his daughter for marrying a gentile but a reconciliation is effected through a coincidental Christmas Eve meeting with a little girl who turns out to be his granddaughter; in *Escaped from Siberia* (1914), a Russian officer is cashiered for his infatuation with a Jewess and, upon his sweetheart's exile to Siberia, he effects their escape to America.

What should one make of these little dramas? Well, for one man's taste, their naiveté had the refreshing charm of the best of primitive art (a charm on the printed page that, admittedly, might have paled on the primitive screen). Their portrait of the Jew was not far from the universal stereotype, though it was far from unflattering. The Jew was seen as a bit of a buffoon (as in *The Airship*), as something of a loser, as the money-lender and the tailor. Yet there was dignity through the suffering, an aura of religiosity and a gentleness.

The prevalent theme of these early motion pictures was the struggle of the poor and innocent. Melodramatically, often panderingly, the nickelodeon spoke to audiences of their sufferings and their hopes to overcome them. The Jews were not seen as separate from this struggle but rather as belonging to and sharing in the common experiences of a much wider cross-current of American life. It would be some time before the film industry would again show the Jew so matter-of-factly a part of American life.

With D. W. Griffith's *The Birth of a Nation* (1915), the movies left its period of infancy. Film was becoming "respectable." Not only were stage actors, previously disdainful of the new medium, lured before the camera's eye, but stage audiences were beginning to pay attention to an entertainment they had earlier relegated to their servants. To encourage this new audience, film promoters built bigger, better, safer theatres and changed the tenor of the screen fare to deal increasingly with more sophisticated levels of society. Screen characters became middle-class or better, losing the traces of their national antecedents; they became, simply, Americans.

There were, to be sure, films that reflected the ethnic heterogeneity of American society—a curious, unassimilated way of life offered to audiences for "local color." Frank Borzage's *Humoresque* (1920) dealt with a Jewish family, the Kantors, who lived in New York's East Side. Mama Kantor (perhaps the first of the screen's *Yiddishe Mamas* with a heart as big as her enormous bosom) wants her son to be a violinist; Papa wants him to learn a useful trade. Mama, of course, wins out, and Sonny becomes a world-famous virtuoso. Sonny, however, gives up his career to (quoting a screen title) "enter a greater world symphony," that of World War I.

The folksiness and bathos of *Humoresque* were a huge success with audiences. Part of this was the film's definite air of taking the audience on a guided tour of the esoteric East Side. Jewish life was shown as some kind of warm, dignified, but definitely strange ritual which the "tourist" (*i.e.,* gentile) could appreciate, even though he could not participate. At the same time, the film reassured, winding up its story by asserting that Jews, however strange their ways, weren't really alien; when the chips were down, they proved themselves American—the Jewish virtuoso shouldering a gun to go to war just like any other Main Street boy.

This dual strand of pointing up the quaintness of immigrant Jewish life and then hastily erasing any suspicions of alien behavior appeared again and again during this period. Another greatly admired film near the end of the silent period was *We Americans* (1928). It exploited the stereotyped characteristics of Jewish, German and Irish families in New York's melting pot, cementing the huge blocks of ethnic kitsch with the continuing theme of their struggles to be good Americans, learning to speak English by attending night school.

Lest one be too condescending to these films, *We Americans* was no worse, no better, than Leo Rosten's much-admired book *The Education of H*Y*M*A*N K*A*P*L*A*N,* while Clifford Odets' play *Golden Boy* was a gutsier but no more profound variation on the theme of *Humoresque.*

One can, however, condescend as much as one likes towards *Abie's Irish Rose* and still be on the side of the angels. This curious theatrical phenomenon opened on Broadway in 1922 to unanimously bad reviews but managed to survive for a staggering 2,327 performances. The play by Anne Nichols dealt with the family uproar created by the marriage of a Jew and a Catholic. It was a compendium of every bad Irish and Jewish joke that ever blemished a vaudeville or burlesque stage. Yet few critics based their criticisms on the insultingly simpering portrait of Jews and Irishmen. They were mostly annoyed by the affront to their funnybone and the old-hat jokes.

The play was filmed for the first time in 1928 with Charles Rogers and Nancy Carroll in the title roles. The film received the same harsh treatment from critics. Refilmed in 1946, the new version was also attacked as "cheap," "banal," "offensive" and "tasteless." Wrote one New York film critic: "The producers are irresponsible, ignorant of their duties as citizens of the Nation and the world, and panderers to anything for a buck." And *Cue Magazine* inveighed against the "distorted echoes and exaggerations of all the cheap racial-accent jokes and leering gags upon religious prejudices that were thrown out of well-run theatres as far back as forty years ago."

Yet the kind of humor exemplified by *Abie's Irish Rose* was a staple of stage and screen well into the 1930s. Only the intrusion of World War II halted a remake of the old chestnut. (When, in the past decade, the civil rights movement became a powerful force, the same strong denunciations were focused on the stereotyped Negro humor as epitomized by Stepin Fetchit, among others, in the 1930s.) It was a crude brand of humor, really more innocent than evil-minded, and in its way reflective of a more relaxed society than the hyper-tense environment that surrounds us today. In retrospect, the relaxation now seems attractive, even if one admits with a pang of guilt that it was bought at the cost of gross indifference.

The huge success of the original *Abie's Irish Rose* bred any number of imitators. The most famous of the film stepchildren was *The Cohens and the Kellys* which starred Jewish comedian George Sidney (who had become famous on stage for his character "Busy Izzy"). So popular was this series that six sequels found *The Cohens and the Kellys* located in *Africa,* in *Hollywood,* in

Paris, etc. (The series continued into the sound era.) The title characters were two business partners, always fighting but, underneath it all, as close as Irish stew is to a *gedempte flaish.* They were described by one critic as the "literary love children of the *Abie's Irish Rose* tradition, and the humor definitely comes from the same mold." An example:

> Kelly: Didn't you ever hear of Daniel in the lion's den?
> Cohen: Yeah, but de lion's den and de lions now ain't de same.

Well, the critics didn't laugh either, although they weren't bothered by the conclusions that might be drawn from such humor, other than the rather obvious fact that audiences really should know better than to laugh at such wince-making gags. But audiences didn't; they laughed and kept laughing through seven films.

Abie's Irish Rose and *The Cohens and the Kellys* placed the ethnic eccentricities upon Old World characters—that is, upon immigrant parents. Abie, Rose and the children of the Cohens and the Kellys were either embarrassed or irritated by their elders' inability to adapt to a new way of life. The elders were figures of fun, the children were the ones made to suffer the weight of reflected ridicule. Once again, it was the national snobbism of "Americanism is best" and the assumption (as in *Humoresque*) that the second generation would knuckle down and divest itself of the quaint ways of the Old Country. And, as is true of even the worst of bad art, there was a kernel of truth here about the contemporary society under scrutiny.

The Biblical spectacle was one of the earliest of all film forms (a version of the Passion Play had been filmed before 1900) and it is one that continues to the present. It would also seem to have had some significant bearing on the theme of Jews in film—but did it really? However much lip service was applied to prove the opposite, the makers of Biblical films were interested less in their inspirational value and the record of Jewish history than they were in spectacle and racy passages.

During the making of *The Queen of Sheba* (1921), an assistant cheekily pointed out to director J. Gordon Edwards that he was going against history by presenting a beardless Solomon. "No motion picture audience would stand for Sheba falling in love with a set of whiskers," Edwards retaliated.

Stripped of their whiskers, the Jews in these films looked just like the Christians or the Romans. The result was that, as in a Western, there were the good guys and the bad guys, the difference having nothing to do with conflicting religious ideologies but rather with who went to the orgies and who didn't.

Cecil B. De Mille was synonymous with the Hollywood Biblical film. The sanest evaluation of his work was given by his niece Agnes De Mille, and much of what she wrote in a magazine article in 1964 fits not only her uncle's work but the Biblical film in general:

> "He has been accused of playing down for box-office reasons. I think he never played down in his life; he believed in everything he did. Therein

lies the secret of his strength. In his own words, 'To transfer the Bible to the screen you cannot cheat. You have to believe.' He chose episodes and characters that proved his point and disregarded whatever did not. He was neither pure nor humble and the people reached were surely not reached at any depth. His Bible stories were never told with the simplicity of revelation, but with the pompous benignity of a 19th century Sunday school teacher. He prided himself on being a profound Biblical scholar and a great part of his career was dedicated to dramatizing and propagandizing the Old Testament, but he never cast a recognizable Jew in any role except to portray villainy."

De Mille was half-Jewish (a fact he never discussed).

The sound era began with Al Jolson singing and Cantor Josef Rosenblatt chanting in *The Jazz Singer* (1927). The film, based on a successful play which had starred George Jessel, told of a musical comedy star who disappoints his father by rejecting the career of a cantor. Once again, a portrait of the older generation clinging stubbornly to traditional ways, while youth showed itself "Americanized" by preferring Broadway to the synagogue.

The Jazz Singer, a landmark in movie technology, was no breakthrough in film depiction of Jews. But it did admit that the Jew existed. In the decade that followed, one had to look fast and hard to find any other film based on Jewish characters. During the 1930s Jewish was *sub rosa* at best, although many of the best Hollywood screenwriters of that period were Jews—Ben Hecht, Arthur Kober, Clifford Odets, Herman Mankiewicz among them—and some were noted for their characterizations of Jewish life in their offscreen writings.

Perhaps Hollywood avoided Jewish themes because it was the safest way to avoid offending anyone. More likely, Hollywood didn't believe that predominantly gentile audiences would sympathize with Jewish heroes and heroines; Jewish was *too special* to be popular. Thus, the unwillingness of some stars (and their studios) to identify a Jewish ancestry. It was common practice for an actor to adopt a screen name if his real one had even the slightest hint of revealing his Jewishness. Jules Garfinkle was a stage actor of reputation before he became the screen's John Garfield. At times, a studio was particularly inventive: MGM let it be known that June Allyson was born Jan Allyson, probably to prevent anyone from digging further to discover that she was really Ella Geisman from the Bronx.

When Hollywood did buy a property that had Jewish overtones, it removed them before bringing it to the screen. On Broadway, Arthur Kober's *Having Wonderful Time* had been a lighthearted comedy about an adults' camp in the Catskill Mountains. In the 1938 screen version, which starred Ginger Rogers and Douglas Fairbanks, Jr., all evidence of its Jewish locale was removed; without the Yiddish tang the film became romantic pap. Similarly, Jerome Weidman's *I Can Get It For You Wholesale,* a novel of New York's Jewish-dominated garment district, became a 1951 movie in which gentile characters replaced the Jewish dress manufacturers. The film version of *The Caine Mutiny* softened Greenwald's Jewish-oriented defense of Captain Queeg and the Jewish family of Arnold Schulman's play *A Hole in the Head* became Italian in the 1959 movie of it. *Marjorie Morningstar*, Herman Wouk's best-selling novel about Bronx Jews who made it to New York's Central Park West, depicted Jewish characters on the screen (1957). But the heroine's universally understood romantic problems dominated and obscured her difficulties of coming to terms with her Jewish ancestry.

Brief flashes of Jewish humor did creep into some of the movies of the 1930s and 40s. The late-late TV movie addict will discover a fleeting Yiddishism in such vehicles as *Three on a Match* (1932), a run-of-the-mill Bette Davis vehicle in which, at a class graduation, a boy fingers the collar of a girl's dress and with the proper inflection remarks, "Nice material"; or in *Her Highness and the Bellboy,* when a bit-player blurts out, "A ticket for speeding he should get!" The appearances of certain actors—an Al Jolson, Eddie Cantor, Ed Wynn, or Fanny Brice (before she succumbed to Baby Snooks)—also, by their mere presence, added an uncommented-on Jewish flavor.

But by and large, Jewish themes were absent. This may have helped along a short-lived Yiddish cinema that began production around New York. The distribution of Yiddish films was limited to big cities with a large enough Yiddish-speaking population to make exhibition profitable. The films ran the whole gamut of subject matter, from such classics as *Mirele Efros* to such lighthearted kitsch as *Yittel with a Fiddle* and *Catskill Honeymoon.* The actors included Maurice Schwartz, Molly Picon, Berta Gerstein, Joseph Buloff, Leo Fuchs and Irving Jacobson. Production of these films petered out in the late 1940s.

By the fall of 1939 the theatre was dealing with the threat of Nazi Germany in a number of advant-garde plays. Talk of Hitler's antisemitism was everywhere, in books, newspapers and magazines, on the radio—everywhere except in the American film. Germany was using movie fiction and documentaries as a powerful propaganda force for pro-Nazism. Hollywood ignored the issue.

Again, the reason was commercial. Hollywood depended strongly on its foreign markets and many films would have shown up in the red were it not for the profits from abroad. (Greta Garbo's exile from the screen originally had less to do with her "I want to be alone" attitude than with the fact that *none* of her films made a profit from their American gross receipts.) Determined to hold on to its foreign markets for as long as possible, Hollywood took care not to offend any foreign country by criticizing its policies. The villains of Robert E. Sherwood's anti-war play *Idiot's Delight,* a Pulitzer Prize winner, were quite definitely Italian and German. When MGM produced it for the screen all mention of specific locale was obscured and the Italian and German in the original dialogue became Esperanto.

A few film efforts contented themselves with historical parallels. Warner Brothers' *The Life of Emile Zola* (1937) used the Dreyfus affair to point up the evils of antisemitism and *Juarez* (1939) told the story of Carlotta and Maximilian's tragic reign in Mexico as a comment upon the iniquities of foreign invasion. But not until World War II was a foregone conclusion and the loss of many foreign markets a certainty, did Hollywood approach the subject of Nazi Germany. Its first effort was *The Mortal Storm,* produced in the 1940s and portraying a Jewish professor (Frank Morgan) who is sent to a concentration camp. His daughter (Margaret Sullavan) and a former student (James Stewart) resist the onslaught of nazism, fall in love, attempt to flee to freedom, but the girl is shot.

The film had a seriousness of purpose and the flaws as well as the pleasures of melodrama. Hollywood, when it did finally turn to the Nazi threat, treated it as new wine poured into old bottles—a novel and topical background for the old clichés of the melodrama and the thriller. Most critics praised *The Mortal Storm* but tempered their kindness with the observation that it was a woefully inadequate treatment of an awesome subject.

Perhaps the only other film of this period which dealt with Nazi antisemitism in any meaningful way was *Tomorrow, the World* (1945). Based on a play by James Gow and Arnaud d'Usseau, its plot was constructed on a Nazi youth who had come to America to live with his uncle. Its thesis, that the American way of life, taught with patience and love, would overcome even the most incalcitrant Nazi indoctrination, was undoubtedly naive. The film's merit was in the character of the uncle's Jewish fiancée, magnificently performed by Betty Field—the most dignified portrait of a Jew in many years.

Following the war, Hollywood entered a sober period in which some of the "big" problems of society came under discussion. (It lasted only a short while: Hollywood was soon made squeamish by the antics of Senator Joe McCarthy and the probes of the House Un-American Activities Committee.) At the top of the agenda was the subject of antisemitism and the first film to deal with it was *Crossfire* (1947) in which a Jew (Sam Levene) is murdered by an antisemite (Robert Ryan). The film was based on a novel, *The Brick Foxhole* by Richard Brooks, whose subject was not antisemitism but intolerance towards homosexuality. In the novel, the victim is a homosexual who had picked up his murderer in a bar. But homosexuality was then a taboo subject for the screen. Since the basic plot of *Crossfire* stemmed from a casual sexual alliance, the film, as a story condemning antisemitism, was not as logical as it should have been. It was, however, powerful and affecting.

A number of critics had strong reservations about it. Wrote Max Lerner: "In *Crossfire,* as in so many 'tolerance' speeches I have heard and on which I am fed up, the big argument given for Protestants and Catholics joining in the fight against antisemitism is that once injustice starts it may spread to them as well, and that they may become its victims. This is the argument of self-interest . . . a morally inadequate argument."

There were some objections also to Elia Kazan's *Gentleman's Agreement* which also appeared that year. Based on Laura Hobson's novel, the film related the experiences of a journalist (Gregory Peck) who passes as a Jew in order to write a series of articles on antisemitism. Most critics agreed that, though dramatically powerful, the film was perhaps too slick and pat, although Lerner compared it favorably to *Crossfire.* "On one important score I am delighted that *Gentleman's Agreement* pulls no punches—the question on which antisemitism must be fought. John Garfield puts it well, when, as a Jewish soldier, he says to his Christian comrade: 'It's your fight, brother. I'm on the side lines . . .' "

Two years later, producer Stanley Kramer brought Arthur Laurents' *Home of the Brave* to the screen. As a play, it dealt with a Jewish G.I. who suffers a mental breakdown, victimized by antisemitic sentiments among his fellow soldiers. In the film the Jew became a Negro. Kramer felt that "the antisemitic angle has been overdone" and he wanted to be first in the Negro sweepstakes. (Two other films released that year—*Pinky* and *Lost Boundaries*—also dealt with Negro themes.) The facile switching of a homosexual to a Jew in *Crossfire* and a Jew to a Negro in *Home of the Brave* pointed up the oversimplified terms in which Hollywood tended to deal with the issue of prejudice. Antisemitism in the military was depicted in the film version of Irwin Shaw's novel *The Young Lions* (1958). The Army refused its cooperation in the making of the film until the script was rewritten to show that the persecutors of the Jewish soldier (Montgomery Clift) had been punished.

The heated dispute that arose over a British production of Charles Dickens' *Oliver Twist* (1948) was more a comment on the sensitivities of the times than on the film itself. The hue and cry from many Jewish groups, protesting the portrayal of Fagin, held up release of the film in the United States for more than two years. John Mason Brown, in *The Saturday Review of Literature,* disputed the attitude of Jews who found Fagin objectionable "not because he is a villain, but because he is a Jewish villain." Brown argued that "for the life of me, I cannot understand how any gentile American who is not a moron or any Jewish American who is not suffering from hallucinations or a persecution mania could discover a provocation for antisemitism in either Fagin as a character or *Oliver Twist* as a film."

Oliver Twist had been filmed three times previously without much objection. Nor was the musical version *Oliver!* (1968) criticized because of Fagin. Interestingly enough, the 1948 film never mentioned that Fagin is Jewish and Alec Guinness, who played him, completely submerged the Jewish characteristics of the role and emphasized the latent homosexuality that can be read into Dickens' character. The strength of Jewish objections led to severe cuts in the 1948 film. Even then its distribution was greatly limited.

The first American film dealing with Israel's statehood was *The Sword in the Desert,* (1952), followed by *The Juggler* (1953), *Exodus* (1960), *Judith* (1965) and *Cast a Giant Shadow* (1966), among others. Most of these used Israel as a novel setting for typical melodramatic exploits of international intrigue and derring-do.

By far, the best was Otto Preminger's *Exodus,* executed with a great deal of panache and professional know-how, and featuring an absolutely irresistible theme song by Ernest Gold. *Exodus* was really an up-dated version of a Biblical spectacle, and like the old De Mille films, it stupefied. With the help of some fresh air on the way from the theatre to their typewriters, a number of critics regained their logic enough to register severe misgivings. They gave it A's as a spectacle, but failed it almost everywhere else. Typical were the words of Amos Elon in Tel Aviv's *Ha'aretz:* "Those who liked the book will like the picture as well; it is the first real Hollywoodian exaggeration of the birth of Israel. Mr. Preminger is feeding his audiences with huge portions of *shmaltz.* Even the most chauvinistic Israeli, even the extremist among Zionists, must feel some resentment. Our historical drama is misrepresented in this picture in a melodramatic way, like in a Western with the Arabs playing the part of the Indians."

During the 1960s there were a number of films that reexamined World War II and its aftermath. George Stevens' *The Diary of Anne Frank* (1960) failed to recreate the impact it had had on the stage because of bad acting, stodgy direction and a wide-screen process that contradicted the feeling of claustrophobia essential to the story. Stanley Kramer's *Judgment at Nuremberg* (1961) was praised by some, but one critic dubbed it "an all-star Concentration Camp Drama with Special Guest Victim Appearances." A flippant remark, but perhaps the crassness of the film deserves it. At one point newsreel footage of the concentration camps was shown, so horrendously real and immediate that it exposed everything that preceded and followed as ineffectual posturing and condescending humanitarian cant. After having witnessed the few moments of actuality, how could an audience be expected to regain its equilibrium in Kramer's tinsely world in which the grotesquely inadequate Judy Garland and Montgomery Clift were meant to stand in for reality?

Of all the American films which touch upon this subject the most effective was Sidney Lumet's *The Pawnbroker* (1965). The film dealt with a former inmate of a concentration camp who, because of his experiences, could no longer participate emotionally in the life around him. Lumet used flash cuts to depict the prisoner's life in the concentration camp—they remained on screen no more than a split second and the effect was to make one *feel* rather than *see.* Consequently the film touched us viscerally, not intellectually; it stirred our nightmarish subconscious of what life in the concentration camps must have been like.

Film has always been the most backward of the arts, following where others had successfully broken ground. By the late 1960s Jewish had become "in." For at least a decade TV comedians had been popularizing Jewish humor and novelists such as Bernard Malamud, Bruce Jay Friedman, Philip Roth and Saul Bellow were making the best-seller lists. Chosen words of *mamaloshen* were *de rigeur* for a sophisticated New Yorker and Barbra Streisand, the last of the

From the motion picture *Goodbye Columbus.* Courtesy of Films Inc.—Paramount.

great, bigger-than-life stars, was the *first* leading lady in the history of Hollywood to wear her Jewishness as in the past a glamour girl would sport a peek-a-boo bob. Hollywood took the hint and started putting the Jewish in where formerly it had taken it out. It would have been unthinkable to bring to the screen Wallace Markfield's novel *To an Early Death,* which concerned not just Jews, but a specific sub-genre, the intellectual Jew, in any other period except the late 1960s. (The film, *Bye, Bye Braverman,* wasn't much of a success, but it wasn't much of a film either.) There are even examples of adding a Jewish tang to material that didn't demand it, as was the case with Mike Nichols' adaptation of Charles Webb's novel, *The Graduate.* Then, at long last, Philip Roth's novella, *Goodbye, Columbus* was brought to the screen.

Goodbye, Columbus was written in 1959. That was my senior year in college and I remember the shock of recognition that spread through the campus as the book was read. The campus was Columbia, with its large Jewish enrollment, but the book was not limited in appeal to any ethnic group. It tapped some hidden nerve in all of us, gentiles and Jews alike; it was to us what F. Scott Fitzgerald's stories must have been (or so we were taught) to our peers of the '20s. For those of us who were film-conscious (amazingly few in light of college students today), it seemed that Roth had written a perfect treatment for a screen scenario.

But *Goodbye, Columbus* wasn't rushed to the screen, undoubtedly because the Hollywood powers felt then that its Jewishness would limit its appeal.

One could counteract this assertion by saying it was the importance a diaphragm plays in the plot that stymied a film producer. Yet this could be refuted by saying that Hollywood had gotten around such essentials in the past. And even so, it could have come to the screen at least three years earlier (remember *The Group?*) when its portrait of youth still might have seemed, if not topical, at least relevant.

By the time *Goodbye, Columbus* and the problems of its heroine Brenda Patimkin reached movie audiences the only thing timely about the film was its satiric treatment of Jews (and in the light of *Portnoy's Complaint* even that seemed old hat). The film had the virtue of fidelity to its original but the original reflected the portrait of the Eisenhower generation, not today's youth. Its strengths were those of Philip Roth, its weaknesses (of which there were many) the fault of its adaptors. The film broadened Roth's satire into burlesque and exhibited a smugness inherent in the attitude of those people who congratulate themselves upon their daring to be in bad taste.

For all the objections *Goodbye, Columbus* was one of those curious landmark films more important than it was good. It was Gertrude Berg turned sour, and yet in that sourness, rested its virtue. Finally, at long last, the kid gloves had been stripped off the treatment of Jews in film. The Jew in the movie had become a full citizen, worthy of taking it on the nose with the worst and the best of us.

So are you ready for *Portnoy's Complaint?*

FOR DISCUSSION

1. The two articles in this section make several observations about stereotyping minority groups in movies and television. Compare the one-dimensional portrayals of American Indians and Jews on the screen with those of Blacks. In what ways are they similar, and how do they differ?

2. Throughout this book we have heard the cries of Blacks criticizing their screen images. Most of them seem agreed that things would be different if Blacks could get a powerful, behind-the-scenes voice in actual film production. Yet, in Gary Carey's article, we discover that Jews have always had powerful voices in film production and still condoned (and encouraged) a one-dimensional portrayal of Jews on the screen (although this stereotype was always sympathetic). The implication is that Jewish film executives were more concerned with a favorable image of their people than a human, realistic one. Discuss this factor in light of all that you have read in this book. Should a minority's goals be concerned with good images or real images? What impact would each portrayal have on mass audiences?

3. Considering the whole complex problem of stereotyping in the "entertainment" industry, discuss what you think is the impact of such distorted presentations on human relations in this country. What other forces foster and nurture prejudice and ignorance? If the entertainment media did treat minorities honestly and realistically, would we have more honest and decent human behavior?

Filmography

Any of the following films can be used profitably as documents on the treatment of Blacks in film. Also available, from Films Incorporated in Wilmette, is a 30-minute, black-and-white compilation reel, featuring extracts from Vincent Minnelli's all-Black *Cabin in the Sky* and Clarence Brown's film adaptation of Faulkner's *Intruder in the Dust.*

INTRODUCTION

Black History: Lost, Stolen, or Strayed. 58 minutes. Color. CBS TV's *Of Black America* Series (narrated by Bill Cosby), 1968. Purchase or rental from Bailey-Film Associates.

SILENT FILMS

One Exciting Night. Directed by D. W. Griffith, 1922. A further example of Griffith's "minstrel show" stereotyping of Blacks. Basically a murder mystery, "comic relief" is provided by a White actor in blackface frightened of the dark. Rental from Museum of Modern Art.
Uncle Tom's Cabin. Available as part of the Edwin S. Porter "package." Directed by Edwin S. Porter, 1903. Rental from Museum of Modern Art. This can only be acquired on a 55-minute reel that includes four other Porter films.
Uncle Tom's Cabin. 93 minutes. Black and white. Directed by Harry Pollard, 1926. This version has a sound track with narration by Raymond Massey. Rental from Audio-Brandon Films.
The Birth of a Nation. 195 minutes. Black and white. Directed by D. W. Griffith (from the novel *The Clansman* by Thomas Dixon), 1915. There is also a 130-minute version available. Rental from Museum of Modern Art.

FEATURED "STEREOTYPES" OF THE 30s, 40s, and 50s

Many of the films with the most blatant examples of the stereotypes I have not been able to find in 16-mm distribution. The following are merely a few suggested titles.

Judge Priest. 80 minutes. Black and white. Directed by John Ford, 1934. A Will Rogers comedy costarring Stepin Fetchit in his stock, stereotyped role. Rental from Films Inc.
Steamboat Round the Bend. 80 minutes. Black and white. Directed by John Ford, 1935. Will Rogers, Stepin Fetchit, and more of the same. Rental from Films Inc.

The Prisoner of Shark Island. 95 minutes. Black and white. Directed by John Ford, 1936. Biographical drama about Dr. Samuel Mudd, who was imprisoned for setting John Wilkes Booth's broken leg after Lincoln's assassination. Includes a sequence in which Black prison guards revolt and are persuaded to give up by the brave Dr. Mudd ("A Southern man who means business"). The Blacks are all portrayed as grotesquely subhuman. Rental from Films Inc.

So Red the Rose. 83 minutes. Black and white. Directed by King Vidor, 1936. The ol' plantation and the Civil War, with "evil" slaves led by Black actor Clarence Muse in revolt. Their rebellion is crushed when their White mistress, Margaret Sullavan, tearfully pleads with them. Rental from Universal 16.

The Littlest Rebel. 80 minutes. Black and white. Directed by David Butler, 1936. Little Shirley Temple teaches her slaves, including Bill Robinson and Willie Best, courage in the face of the Yankee invaders. Rental from Films Inc.

Ghost Breakers. 85 minutes. Black and white. Directed by George Marshall, 1940. Standard Bob Hope comedy, with Willie Best, for laughs, caught in a haunted house. This was a standard gag scene for many Black film actors. Rental from Universal 16.

Virginia. 109 minutes. Black and white. Directed by Edmund H. Griffith, 1941. Modern times force the break-up of the ol' plantation. Loaded with nostalgia and "darky" stereotypes. Rental from Universal 16.

The Charlie Chan Series. 1931-1949. This series of films about the Chinese detective (himself a stereotype) had many episodes involving Chan's Black chauffeur, Mantan Moreland, who was noted for his ability to roll his eyes to show fear. Many of these are available, and I recommend their use. They represent America's stereotyping of minorities at its most explicit level. Check local film exchanges for rental.

The Oxbow Incident. 76 minutes. Black and white. Directed by William Wellman, 1943. A well-known, excellent film about mob "justice," it includes an interesting Black character—Sparks, an itinerant preacher. Played by Leigh Whipper, Sparks by speaking against the mob and praying for the souls of the accused men serves as a kind of conscience for Whites. This is a new kind of stereotype, which would be repeated often in later films. Rental from Films Inc. and Audio-Brandon Films.

Bend of the River. 91 minutes. Color. Directed by Anthony Mann, 1952. A popular James Stewart Western, featuring Stepin Fetchit in what was probably his last standard role. Rental from Universal 16.

WAR PROPAGANDA FILMS WITH BLACK ACTORS

Lifeboat. 97 minutes. Black and white. Directed by Alfred Hitchcock, 1944. Canada Lee, as one of the survivors, in this famous film. Lee is somewhat removed from the negative stereotype. Rental from Films Inc.

Bataan. 93 minutes. Black and white. Directed by Tay Garnett, 1943. The doomed soldiers of this famous battle have among them a distinguished, heroic Black comrade, Kenneth Spencer. This film was made at the beginning of World War II, and its propaganda was extremely effective. Rental from Films Inc.

Sahara. 97 minutes. Black and white. Directed by Zoltan Korda, 1943. A classic war film, with Humphrey Bogart, about a group of men (including a Black Libyan soldier played by Rex Ingram) trapped by Germans in North Africa. Their courage persists, and the Black is among the most heroic. Actor Ingram later played Uncle Remus in Disney's *Song of the South.* Rental from Audio-Brandon Films.

The Green Berets. 141 minutes. Color. Directed by John Wayne and Ray Kellogg, 1968. Wayne's cliché-ridden propaganda film for the Vietnam War features a brave Black man, Raymond St. Jacques. St. Jacques later admitted that he was ashamed of the movie. Rental from Audio-Brandon Films.

ALL-BLACK FEATURES

Hallelujah. 107 minutes. Black and white. Directed by King Vidor, 1929. Rental from Films Inc.

The Green Pastures. 110 minutes. Black and white. Directed by Marc Connelly and William Keighly, 1936. Rental from Films Inc. and United Artists 16.

Cabin in the Sky. 100 minutes. Black and white. Directed by Vincent Minnelli, 1943. Rental from Films Inc.

Carmen Jones. 107 minutes. Color (cinemascope print available). Directed by Otto Preminger, 1955. Rental from Films Inc.

Porgy and Bess. 138 minutes. Color. Directed by Otto Preminger, 1959. Rental from Audio-Brandon Films.

SOCIAL DRAMAS CONCERNING BLACKS

This grouping excludes the Sidney Poitier films. Notice how few there are without him.

Lost Boundaries. 99 minutes. Black and white. Directed by Alfred L. Werker, 1949. The male version of *Pinky*. Rental from Warner Brothers 16.

Pinky. 102 minutes. Black and white. Directed by Elia Kazan, 1949. Rental from Films Inc.

Home of the Brave. 85 minutes. Black and white. Directed by Mark Robson, 1949. Rental from Audio-Brandon Films and Twyman Films.

Intruder in the Dust. 87 minutes. Black and white. Directed by Clarence Brown, 1949. Rental from Films Inc.

Island in the Sun. 119 minutes. Color. Directed by Robert Rossen, 1957. Terrible film about a couple of interracial romances in Jamaica. It's hard to believe this stuff was once considered daring. With Harry Belafonte and Dorothy Dandridge as the exotic objects of White appetites. Rental from Films Inc.

Odds Against Tomorrow. 95 minutes. Black and white. Directed by Robert Wise, 1959. A robbery melodrama involving the animosity between two of the gang members: a fierce bigot (Robert Ryan) and a Black (Harry Belafonte). The film has a pretentious air, but Belafonte's role has quite a bit of depth. Still, because he is Black, he is somehow made more noble than the rest of the thieves. Rental from United Artists 16.

Imitation of Life. 124 minutes. Color. Directed by Douglas Sirk, 1959. A remake of the 1934 film about a family, its loyal maid, and her mulatto daughter who passes for White. This film brings back all of the female stereotypes in the portrayal of that maid. The original version is also available in 16 mm. This one is recommended only to show how recently (1959) Blacks have been dramatized this way. Rental of both versions from Universal 16.

Shadows. 81 minutes. Black and white. Directed by John Cassavetes, 1960. I have not seen Cassavetes' improvisational film about an interracial romance, but I have been informed that it deals with its subject honestly. Rental from Audio-Brandon Films.

Gone Are the Days (Purlie Victorious). 97 minutes. Black and white. Directed by Nicholas Webster, 1963. The film version of Ossie Davis's hilarious satire *Purlie Victorious.* In this film the stereotypes serve an excellent satirical purpose. Rental from Audio-Brandon Films.

The Cool World. 104 minutes. Black and white. Directed by Shirley Clarke, 1964. A devastating, realistic portrait of a Harlem juvenile gang leader. A good film to contrast to the sentimental stereotypes of the social drama genre. Rental from Zipporah Films.

Nothing But a Man. 92 minutes. Black and white. Directed by Michael Roemer, 1963. A brilliant film, honestly portraying a Black couple's struggle for survival in today's South. The best of the genre. Rental from Audio-Brandon Films.

One Potato, Two Potato. 92 minutes. Black and white. Directed by Larry Peerce, 1964. A sometimes overly sentimental drama about racial intermarriage. Still it does not patronize Blacks. Rental from Twyman Films or Swank Films.

The Comedians. 160 minutes. Color (cinemascope print available). Directed by Peter Glenville, 1967. This film version of Graham Greene's best seller about modern Haiti is badly hurt by a murky Elizabeth Taylor-Richard Burton romance. But the Black supporting actors are great, and their roles are complex and dignified. With James Earl Jones, Raymond St. Jacques, and Roscoe Lee Brown. Rental from Films Inc.

The Scalphunters. 102 minutes. Color. Directed by Sidney Pollack, 1968. A Western that treats the race issue humorously as a rugged frontiersman (Burt Lancaster) and a brilliant runaway slave (Ossie Davis) team up to fight a band of renegade outlaws. Unrealistic, but funny, and the Black character is really "alive." Rental from United Artists 16.

Joanna. 107 minutes. Color (cinemascope print available). Directed by Michael Sarne, 1968. A pretentious film about a "mod" London "chick," who falls in love with a Black man. It is interesting only since its portrayal of the lover by Calvin Lockhart is in the typical matinée idol vein (kind of a Black Paul Newman). Rental from Films Inc.

Slaves. 110 minutes. Color. Directed by Herbert Biberman, 1969. This film was supposed to be the first honest look at American slavery. Although the Blacks are the "good guys," *Slaves* is merely a one-dimensional piece of sentimentality. It's like a film version of a William Lloyd Garrison speech. Everybody, Black and White, is stereotyped. View this to see how little movies have changed, despite its more pro-Black approach. Rental from Walter Reade 16.

Up Tight. 104 minutes. Color. Directed by Jules Dassin, 1968. The movies' first portrayal of Black power. This film is only partially successful. It is really a remake of the Irish classic *The Informer,* and the parallels of the two rebellions aren't exact enough to justify this interpretation. Still its characters are vividly depicted and performed. Rentals from Films Inc.

Halls of Anger. 100 minutes. Color. Directed by Paul Bogart, 1970. Here is a film with lots of Black actors, all competent (especially Calvin Lockhart in the lead). They are young and angry and quite in keeping with the film's plot about a Black high school about to be integrated by some Whites. However, though the characterizations are adequate, the story line is so exaggerated and badly directed that the Blacks emerge looking like vicious savages. (There is one scene of some Black students brutally beating a White girl without the slightest provocation. This is rude sensationalism at best.) Rental from United Artists 16.

THE SIDNEY POITIER "STEREOTYPE"

Listed here are the actor's better-known films in chronological order, according to what is available in 16 mm. It is important to note that most of the racial dramas of the past two decades feature Poitier. Few other Black actors had his opportunities. Class discussion on these films should go beyond their content and deal with the tokenism of Hollywood in this respect. It should also question whether or not the new stereotype accusations are true.

No Way Out. 106 minutes. Black and white. Directed by Joseph L. Mankiewicz, 1950. Poiter as a Black doctor who is tormented by a racist (Richard Widmark). In the end, loyal to his profession, he must save the racist's life. Rental from Films Inc.

The Blackboard Jungle. 101 minutes. Black and white. Directed by Richard Brooks, 1955. This is still a powerful film about a teacher in a tough slum school. Gregory Miller, a Black student, tough and bitter, in the end helps the teacher win over the class. One of Poitier's best acting jobs. Rental from Films Inc.

Edge of the City. 85 minutes. Black and white. Directed by Martin Ritt, 1956. A White wanderer (John Cassavetes) learns about humanity from his Black coworker (Sidney Poitier). The Black man is murdered by a racist and his White friend avenges it by beating up the killer. He thus learns the "meaning of life." This is a tough melodrama, but the Black man's role is that of conscience to the Whites. He is that spirit-like character of the war propaganda films and the *Oxbow Incident.* Rental from Films Inc.

The Defiant Ones. 97 minutes. Black and white. Directed by Stanley Kramer, 1958. A classic film about two convicts, one White (Tony Curtis), one Black (Poitier), who escape from a work camp, symbolically chained together. In the end, Poitier sacrifices his chance for freedom to aid his White comrade—a role, author Clifford Mason claims, he has played too often. Rental from United Artists 16.

All the Young Men. 87 minutes. Black and white. Directed by Hal Bartlett, 1960. A Korean War film about a Black sergeant and a tough veteran member of the outfit competing for the men's affection. Later when the White is wounded, a blood transfusion really binds the men together. Pretentious. Rental from Twyman Films or Swank Films.

Paris Blues. 98 minutes. Black and white. Directed by Martin Ritt, 1961. Paul Newman and Sidney Poitier as two American jazz musicians in Paris who meet two female tourists (Joanne Woodward and Diahann Carroll). Though the film has little plot, the romance between Poitier and Miss Carroll is nicely developed, and except for *A Raisin in the Sun,* it marks the actor's first screen attachment to a woman. Rental from United Artists 16.

A Raisin in the Sun. 127 minutes. Black and white. Directed by Daniel Petrie, 1961. Lorraine Hansberry's classic drama adapted for the screen gave Poitier one of his most human roles. Rental from Audio-Brandon Films, Twyman Films, or Swank Films.

Pressure Point. 89 minutes. Black and white. Directed by Hubert Cornfield, 1962. Good psychological study of an American Nazi (Bobby Darin) in the care of a Black psychiatrist. Rental from United Artists 16.

Lilies of the Field. 97 minutes. Black and white. Directed by Ralph Nelson, 1963. Poitier's Oscar-winning performance as a wandering handyman who helps some refugee nuns build a chapel in the Arizona desert. This film is very entertaining, but it marks the beginning of the actor's evolution into "I serve" parts. Rental from Audio-Brandon Films.

The Long Ships. 125 minutes. Color. Directed by Jack Cardiff, 1964. A run-of-the-mill adventure about some Vikings lost in an African empire. Poitier plays a villainous sultan, and although he has since denounced the role as a mistake, critic Clifford Mason in his *New York Times* article implies it is a milestone for a Black actor. Check local film exchanges for rental.

The Bedford Incident. 102 minutes. Black and white. Directed by James B. Harris, 1965. Poitier plays a reporter on board an atomic submarine commanded by a fanatical captain bent on starting an atomic war. Critic Mason argues that the Poitier role as critic of the captain is too weakly written. I see it as the stereotyped "conscience" of the ship, the "holier than thou" spirit that Blacks must assume among sinful Whites. Rental from Audio-Brandon Films.

Duel at Diablo. 103 minutes. Color. Directed by Ralph Nelson, 1966. A far-fetched Western that has the dubious distinction of making Poitier the first gun-toting Black cowboy in screen history. (Actually actor Frank Silvera had been playing such parts for years, but as a White man or a Mexican.) Otherwise his role is merely sidekick to hero James Garner. Rental from United Artists 16.

To Sir with Love. 105 minutes. Color. Directed by James Clavell, 1967. Sentimental story of a Black teacher in a White British slum school. There are some suggestions of a possible romance with a White teacher, but they are brushed aside. This film was very successful. Rental from Twyman Films or Swank Films.

In the Heat of the Night. 109 minutes. Color. Directed by Norman Jewison, 1967. This film won the Academy Award, as did actor Rod Steiger for his portrayal of a tough, but sympathetic Southern police chief. Poitier plays a Northern cop on leave, who singlehandedly solves a notorious crime. Mr. Mason's article is particularly critical of the one-dimensional nature of the role. Rental from United Artists 16.

Guess Who's Coming to Dinner. 108 minutes. Color. Directed by Stanley Kramer, 1968. The story of parents' (Spencer Tracy and Katherine Hepburn) reaction to their daughter's betrothal to a Black man. Their future son-in-law is a superhuman figure. (Nobel prize-winning surgeon, missionary, decorated by the U. N., etc.) This film is highly controversial despite its light treatment of the subject (it is supposed to be a comedy), since many Blacks are upset by Poitier's role. They claim the whole thing is racist, since a man of his stature shouldn't have to humble himself to ask for the hand of a silly White teenager (Katherine Houghton). Screen this film in light of today's widening polarity between the races and see how you react. Rental from Twyman Films or Swank Films.

BLACK FILM-MAKERS—A NEW BREED

The Story of a Three Day Pass. 87 minutes. Black and white. Directed by Melvin Van Peebles (French). 1967. English subtitles. This film, although produced in French, is the first commercial feature ever directed by a Black man, Melvin Van Peebles. Its story of a Black GI's brief romance with a Parisian girl leaves much to be desired, but the characterization is honest, and Van Peebles has made an important breakthrough. Rental from Audio-Brandon Films.

Sweet Sweetback's Baadasss Song. 97 minutes. Color. Directed by Melvin Van Peebles, 1971. A controversial, highly adult film about a Black fugitive's attack at "the man." Little plot and dialogue, yet the whole film is orchestrated for a Black audience to "groove" with it. An example of a possible "new cinema" for Blacks. Rated X. Rental from Warner Brothers Film Gallery.

Cotton Comes to Harlem. 90 minutes. Color. Directed by Ossie Davis, 1970. A riotous "Black" comedy based on Chester Himes' novel about two tough Black cops. The film is refreshing for its soul brother point of view and it is loaded with "inside" jokes. *Cotton* represents a great step forward in the portrayal of Blacks as human beings. Rental from United Artists 16.

The Learning Tree. 107 minutes. Color. Directed by Gordon Parks, 1969. Parks' memoir of his youth in the middle west. Interesting personal film, from a Black point of view, but somewhat slow moving. Rental from Twyman Films or Swank Films.

Shaft. 98 minutes. Color. Directed by Gordon Parks, 1971. The Black film-maker's version of the private eye myth. Loaded with hip racial commentary and violence. Rental from Films Inc.

SELECTED 16 MM FILM RENTAL LIBRARIES

Audio-Brandon Films. 34 MacQuesten Parkway So., Mount Vernon, N. Y. 10550. Tel.: (914) 664-5051. *Branches:* 2138 East 7th St., Chicago, Ill. 60649. Tel.: (312) MU 4-2531. 406 Clement St., San Francisco, Calif. 94118. Tel.: (415) SK 2-4800.

Bailey Film Associates. 6509 De Longpre Ave., Hollywood, Calif. 90028. Tel.: (213) 466-4331.

Films Inc.—9 offices, regionally. 1) 227 Pharr Road, N. E., Atlanta, Ga. 30305. Tel.: (404) 237-0341. (Georgia, Alabama, Florida, Mississippi, North and South Carolina, and Tennessee.) 2) 161 Massachusetts Ave., Boston, Mass. 02115. Tel.: (617) 937-1110. (Massachusetts, Connecticut, Maine, New Hampshire, Rhode Island, and Vermont.) 3) 1414 Dragon St., Dallas, Tex. 75207. Tel.: (214) 741 4071. (Texas, Arkansas, Louisiana, New Mexico, and Oklahoma.) 4) 5625 Hollywood Blvd., Hollywood, Calif. 90028. Tel:. (213) 466-5481. (California, Arizona, Colorado, Nevada, Utah, and Wyoming.) 5) 3501 Queens Blvd., Long Island City, N. Y. Tel.: (212) 937-1110. (New

York, New Jersey, Delaware, Maryland, Pennsylvania, Virginia, and Washington, D. C.) 6) 2129 N. E. Broadway, Portland, Oreg. 97232. Tel.: (503) 282-5558. (Oregon, Idaho, Montana, and Washington.) 7) 44 East South Temple, Salt Lake City, Utah. Tel.: (801) 328-8191. (Utah and Idaho.) 8) 3034 Canon St. (Kerr Film Exchange), San Diego, Calif. Tel.: (714) 224-2406. (San Diego Metropolitan Area) 9) 4420 Oakton St., Skokie, Ill. 60076. Tel.: (312) 676-1088 (Skokie), (312) 583-3330 (Chicago). (Illinois, Indiana, Iowa, Kansas, Kentucky, Michigan, Minnesota, Missouri, Nebraska, North and South Dakota, West Virginia, and Ohio.)

Museum of Modern Art, Department of Film Circulating Programs. 11 West 53rd St., New York, N. Y. 10022. Tel.: (212) 245-8900.

Swank Motion Pictures. 201 South Jefferson Ave., St. Louis, Mo. 63166. Tel.: (314) 531-5100.

Twyman Films. 329 Salem Ave., Dayton, Ohio 45401. Tel.: (513) 222-4014.

United Artists 16. 729 Seventh Ave., New York, N. Y. 10019. Tel.: (212) 245-6000.

Universal 16. 221 Park Ave. So., New York, N. Y. 10003. Tel.: (212) 777-6600.

Walter Reade 16. 241 East 34th St., New York, N. Y. 10016. Tel.: (212) 683-6300.

Warner Brothers 16. 666 Fifth Ave., New York, N. Y. 10019. Tel.: (212) 246-1000.

Zipporah Films. 54 Lewis Wharf, Boston, Mass. 02110. Tel.: (617) 742-6680.